Wel

Holy Spirit with

Padre Pio

MW00774704

"*Welcoming the Holy Spirit with Padre Pio* is an engrossing meditation on the life of Padre Pio. Susan De Bartoli masterfully sets the historical and spiritual drama by drawing upon the private prayer life and letters of Padre Pio as well as firsthand accounts of his life and works. This book is perfect for those unacquainted with this modern mystic, for those who are looking to grow deeper in their devotion to him, and for families who are looking for a spiritual resource that will engage all ages in fruitful conversation."

Alex Dee
Cofounder and director
Saints Alive Podcast

"De Bartoli's devotion, love, and knowledge of Padre Pio shine through her writing. *Welcoming the Holy Spirit with Padre Pio* is a great read for anyone looking to understand more about how Padre Pio lived in two worlds: the physical and the spiritual."

Nicholas Salkowski
Director of Communications
National Centre for Padre Pio

"De Bartoli's book takes you on a unique journey. The captivating stories she shares guide you through the diverse aspects of Padre Pio's life. The book not only delves into Padre Pio's personal experiences but also encourages readers to look at them through the lens of their own lives. Padre Pio's life was marked by profound suffering yet also immense love and compassion. By the end of this book, you will have gained a deeper understanding of Padre Pio, his many gifts, and his devotion and love for Jesus Christ."

Julie Fitts Ritter
Executive Director
Padre Pio Foundation of America

"This book helps us to unveil the mystery of Padre Pio's spiritual gifts and struggles while enkindling in us personal conversion. It offers deeper insights into the life of this beloved twenty-first-century saint while encountering a new invitation to holiness. A pilgrimage in writing."

Jana Zuniga
Owner
January Jane Shop

Welcoming the Holy Spirit with Padre Pio

Susan De Bartoli

Ave Maria Press AVE Notre Dame, Indiana

Nihil Obstat:	Reverend Monsignor Michael Heintz, PhD
	Censor Librorum
Imprimatur:	Most Reverend Kevin C. Rhoades
	Bishop of Fort Wayne–South Bend
	Given at Fort Wayne, Indiana, on 2 November 2023

$\mathcal{C}$ONTENTS

Introduction: How Deep Is Your Well? **ix**

1. A River of Living Water **1**

2. Padre Pio's Early Life and Visitations **11**

3. The Spiritual Gifts Revealed **19**

4. Mystical Touches **31**

5. Winds of Change **39**

6. Five Million Confessions **49**

7. Persecution and Confinement **63**

8. Protection in Wartime **83**

9. Maria L'Americana **93**

10. Padre Pio's Dream **103**

11. Miracles and Recollections **113**

12. The Journey Home **131**

Notes **139**

How Deep Is Your Well?

A recurring theme in this book is a true question of faith. If faith is like a well that is filled with the Living Water, Jesus, who through the Spirit gives us every good gift, we must ask ourselves one simple question: *How deep is our well?*

Every day, do we return to draw that Living Water from the well and share it with others? This was Padre Pio's life in a nutshell. His life flowed like a river of Living Water out into the world, for he was always connected to the one true source of that water, Jesus. By the time Padre Pio was five years old, his well was already overflowing. Throughout his life, he helped thousands of people to turn to God, showing them the path to sainthood, the road to paradise.

How deep is *your* well? As you read about the life and gifts of Padre Pio, that is the question you must answer for yourself. As you read this book, listen with the ears of your heart to what the Holy Spirit is saying to you. Let him lead you, too, to the Living Water that feeds our well of faith. Let us continually return to that well with a heart of simple humility, to draw the fresh, pure water of faith.

This book shares the story of how Padre Pio drew deeply from his own well of faith even in his darkest hours, especially during his years of confinement. By his own example, he shows us how to trust in the Lord to help us in our darkest hours.

MY FIRST IMPRESSIONS

Padre Pio is one of the most remarkable figures in the history of the Catholic Church, especially in the twentieth century. After World War II, Padre Pio became a household name for many American families. The American soldiers who met Padre Pio during the war brought back incredible stories about the monk who lived on a mountain. These young soldiers were enthralled by him, and many said they believed that he protected them in battle. Some of them—like my friend Ray Ewen—served Mass with Padre Pio.

Many of these soldiers experienced Padre Pio's extraordinary mystical gifts firsthand. Some said that he predicted their futures—when they would marry, what their careers would be, and even that some would become priests. Two such soldiers went on to become Capuchins.

Although I became aware of Padre Pio at an early age, it wasn't until 1995—long after his death—that I visited San Giovanni Rotondo for the first time. My experience there led me to a deep devotion for this amazing monk. Padre Pio is truly a man for our times. Investigating his numerous miracles leads us to a simple, humble man, a holy man, a man who left us with the words, "Pray, hope, and don't worry." These are words he wished us to live by. Words he certainly lived himself.

THE EARLY LIFE OF PADRE PIO

On May 25, 1887, Francesco Forgione (Padre Pio) was born to Grazio and Maria Giuseppa Forgione. Francesco lived a simple Christian life. He was only five years old when he began to contemplate consecrating his life to God.

Francesco was a quiet child who loved to go to church and pray. As a young boy, he could see and communicate with his guardian angel and also with Jesus and the Virgin Mary. He began to experience ecstasies and apparitions when he was just five years of age, but for a long time he did not tell anyone about them. When Padre Pio was asked why he did not tell anyone about the visions he was receiving, he replied, "I believed that these things happened to everybody."[1]

When we hear about miracles and extraordinary occurrences, most of us are understandably skeptical, at least initially. Yet somehow the stories of Padre Pio—many of which include unusual mystical experiences—are often met with curiosity rather than skepticism. Why is that?

I think the miracles associated with Padre Pio's ministry intrigue us, but it is the simplicity of his faith that keeps us coming back. How did such a humble man cause such a sensation in the world?

We need to move forward in Padre Pio's life to see how this happened and how Our Lord and Our Lady prepared him for the extraordinary life he would lead.

The Mystical Gifts of Padre Pio

Throughout his life, Padre Pio used his gifts to bless and encourage those who came to him for assistance. And yet the gifts also fortified him for an interior battle that the Lord entrusted to him as a teenager. In September 1899, Francesco received his first Holy Communion and Confirmation, and soon after he received an inner warning of the struggles he would have to endure in combating evil. He would have to choose a path to follow, a decision that was illuminated for him by the delicate touch of grace.

The celebration of Mass was the center of Padre Pio's spirituality. His Masses sometimes lasted for several hours and were truly the living Passion of Christ. His parish priest in Pietrelcina called Padre Pio's Mass "an incomprehensible mystery."[2]

On September 20, 1918, while praying in the choir loft of the Church of Santa Maria delle Grazie, Padre Pio received the stigmata, the wounds of Christ. Along with the stigmata came remarkable spiritual gifts, including healing, bilocation, and prophecy. When asked about these gifts, he replied, "You know, they are a mystery to me, too."[3] Padre Pio never felt worthy of these gifts. He always remained humble.

One reason that Padre Pio's faith was so strong and that his prayers were answered in sometimes miraculous ways was that his whole life was one of prayer and wholehearted, simple service to Jesus and his mother. Padre Pio loved to pray the Rosary and recommended it to others. If someone asked what legacy he wished to leave to his spiritual children, he would reply, "My child, the Rosary."

Padre Pio placed himself and everything he possessed in the hands of the Lord. He would deprive himself of simple things just so there would be more room in his heart for Jesus. He never wanted or expected a thank you. All he did he did for the Lord.

Padre Pio's confessor and spiritual director, Padre Agostino Daniele, once said, "One must admire his habitual union with God."[4] At all times and in all conversation, Padre Pio was never far from his thoughts of God.

About This Book

This book provides a unique opportunity to meet one of the most extraordinary saints in the history of the Catholic Church, especially in the modern era. First as a child, then as a man, Padre Pio walked in the footsteps of the

Lord. He spent his life defending the Lord and fighting the devil, day and night.

Padre Pio was a man of great faith. He put everything in God's hands. He lived the words he gave us: "Pray, hope, and don't worry." Have faith! Give it all to God! Where did this great faith come from? From his earliest days Padre Pio drew from the well of the Living Water, the Lord. As he grew, so did his love for the Lord. He lived for the Lord alone. From the beginning, the Living Water welled up in his soul until he became a river, flowing out to others.

As we journey through Padre Pio's life, we will see his river overflow. We will meet the humble intercessor whose prayers brought great miracles to simple, ordinary people. We will hear about his ecstasies and apparitions, and we will experience his constant battle with the devil.

Most of all, we will meet the Holy Spirit through Padre Pio's spiritual gifts. These gifts will come to life, and we will see things that we may question. Then we must stop and ask ourselves . . .

How deep is your well?

Join me on this remarkable journey with Padre Pio to the gates of paradise. He is waiting there for you.

$\mathscr{A}$ River of Living Water

> Always humble yourself lovingly before God and man,
> because God speaks to those who are truly humble of
> heart and enriches them with his gifts.
>
> —Padre Pio

Faith is like a well full of water. The deeper the well, the cooler the water, and the more refreshed we will be. Our Lord is the Living Water who resides in the well of our souls. The stronger our faith, the deeper the well, and the more refreshed our souls. To receive this gift of Living Water, we only need to follow him.

Remember the story in the Gospel of John about Jesus and the Samaritan woman at the well? When he encounters her drawing water at high noon, Jesus asks the Samaritan woman for water. She responds, "How can you, a Jew, ask me, a Samaritan woman, for a drink?"(Jn 4:9).

How does Jesus answer her? "If you knew the gift of God and who is saying to you, 'Give me a drink,' you would have asked him and he would have given you living water" (Jn 4:10).

How deep is your well?

Padre Pio's well was far deeper than most. The bucket that we lower into our well would not touch the ripples on Padre Pio's water! The richness of his faith was evident in his everyday life. Through Padre Pio's spiritual gift of tears alone, he could fill a well.

THE GIFT OF TEARS

One of God's most fearless warriors, King David, wrote in Psalm 56, "My wanderings you have noted; are my tears not stored in your flask, recorded in your book?" (v. 9). In so many words, he notes that God cares about the struggles and sufferings of those who follow him and seek to do his will. Although the gift of tears is not referenced specifically in the Bible, there is a long-standing mystical tradition in which tears are a sign of a deep and powerful encounter with God. This was certainly the case with Padre Pio.

Padre Pio's tears were involuntary, flowing continually as a sign of his love for God. Just thinking about his love for the Lord often brought Padre Pio to tears. In fact, Padre Pio said, "Tears are my daily bread!" He lived and suffered for the Lord, and through these tears, he showed the Lord the depths of his love and the yearning in his soul to be with the Lord.

As a child, Padre Pio experienced the presence of the Lord in his everyday life. While other children played, he spent his days in sweet conversation with the Lord and Our Lady.

Have you ever felt a sense of the Lord's presence so strongly that it moved you to tears? If so, then you know something of Padre Pio's experience. From the time he was very young, he loved God and wanted to be near him.

A LIFELONG CONSECRATION

One of Padre Pio's spiritual directors said that Padre Pio was just five years old when he began to consider the idea of dedicating himself to God forever.

Padre Pio shared many childhood stories with his spiritual son Fr. Giuseppe Caccioppoli. On one occasion, he told Fr. Caccioppoli that he had experienced the visible companionship of his guardian angel since infancy. On another occasion, he told Fr. Caccioppoli about his first meeting with Jesus. He said that one day he did not feel like playing with the other kids in front of the church and decided to go in and sit down in a pew. Jesus then gestured to him from the tabernacle to approach the altar and put his hand on the boy's head.[1]

This was Padre Pio's first personal contact with the Lord. How old was the boy Francesco when Jesus invited him to the altar? He doesn't say, but it would seem he was quite young since we know he was ready to consecrate himself to God at the age of five.

Padre Pio's mother described Francesco as a quiet child who loved to go to church and pray.[2] And his spiritual director at San Marco in Lamis, Padre Agostino Daniele, said that as a young boy Francesco saw and communicated with not only his guardian angel but also Jesus and the Virgin Mary. This explains Padre Pio's great affection for Jesus, Our Lady, and his guardian angel. It seems that from childhood Padre Pio had heavenly visitations.

In later years, after he entered the seminary, Fr. Tarcisio of Cervinara asked Padre Pio, "When did you start suffering?" Padre Pio responded, "From the time I was in my mother's womb."[3] There is no question that Padre Pio walked with the Lord all his life. From his earliest childhood he spoke to Jesus and his Blessed Mother.

Padre Pio's mother taught him to pray the Rosary at a young age. On many occasions, Francesco chose to pray the Rosary rather than play. In addition, his family prayed the Rosary together every day. As a priest, Padre Pio often urged people to pray to Our Lady, who was a great intercessor. He would say, "My child, pray the Rosary." To Jesus through Mary!

Are You Drinking Living Water?

In all his words and actions, Padre Pio tells us to drink deeply from the Living Water. Over and over the scriptures call us to quench our thirst by drinking deeply from the Living Water in our well of faith:

- Speaking to the Samaritan woman, Jesus said, "Whoever drinks the water I shall give will never thirst; the water I shall give will become in him a spring of water welling up to eternal life" (Jn 4:14).
- In John 7, we hear the Lord's invitation, "Whoever believes in me, as scripture says: 'Rivers of living water will flow from within him'" (Jn 7:38).
- In the very last book of the Bible, Revelation, Jesus proclaims on the last and greatest day of the feast, "Let the one who thirsts come forward, and the one who wants it receive the gift of life-giving water" (Rv 22:17).

In each of these passages, Jesus is referring to the Spirit that those who come to believe in him will receive. So, by telling us to drink of the Living Water, Jesus is instructing us to welcome the Holy Spirit, from whom we receive all spiritual gifts by virtue of our baptism. Like Padre Pio, each of us must accept the Lord's invitation to drink the Living Water and thus meet the Holy Spirit on the roadway to heaven.

Of course, the path that Padre Pio chose to follow in life was different from ours. He was a simple, humble man who in a spirit of love dedicated his whole life to Jesus, even to the point of embracing the stigmata. What does that mean?

THE STIGMATA OF PADRE PIO

The stigmata are mystical and often physical manifestations of the wounds that Jesus received on the Cross. You will recall that the hands, feet, and side of Jesus were pierced by the Roman soldiers who crucified him. Throughout the history of the Church, there have been saints who have received a special mystical touch from God, which allows them to carry on their bodies these marks of the Passion, to help them identify more completely with Christ.

Padre Pio bore the stigmata for fifty years. Every day of his life during those fifty years, he suffered the Passion of the Lord—the unimaginable pain that Jesus felt when he was crucified. This pain was especially evident when Padre Pio celebrated Mass. At times the pain in his feet was unbearable, and he needed to lean on the altar in order to continue saying Mass.

Padre Pio's path was difficult. In comparison, ours is not! In our search we do not need to suffer as Padre Pio did. We only need to reflect on this journey of Padre Pio. For us, the road will be easier. We will find the Lord in the spiritual gifts that Padre Pio received, and we will glimpse his humility in the miracles received through his intercession.

Each of us receives spiritual gifts to help us go deeper into the well to experience the presence of the Lord in our lives. Padre Pio had his first personal encounter with God when he was a little child. This awareness of God's presence led him to the Capuchin monastery of Morcone at the age of fifteen.

For each of us, the ways we encounter Christ on the road to heaven will be different. Perhaps you have never stopped to consider the spiritual gifts you received at baptism, which continued to grow in you at Confirmation. These gifts are wisdom and understanding, counsel and fortitude, knowledge and piety, and fear of the Lord. These gifts continue to bear fruit in our lives—love and joy and peace, patience and gentleness and self-control. We will surely receive an increase of these gifts on this journey together.

As you read about the gifts of Padre Pio, and all the ways he helped his spiritual sons and daughters to follow Jesus, you will have a chance to think about your own spiritual gifts and find new ways to get close to Jesus as together we walk the path toward heaven. Let us follow Padre Pio, the river of Living Water. He will lead us to the source of the Living Water, the Lord, and as we drink from his graces our souls will be refreshed. Do you have the faith to follow this path to heaven?

How deep is your well?

REFLECTION

Today and every day we find ourselves taking one more step on our journey toward heaven. Our guide is Padre Pio. This man of deep faith will show us how to receive the Living Water in our souls.

How is it that Padre Pio was able to endure the stigmata for fifty years? We find the answer in the graces he received from God. Padre Pio was a man who was continually touched by the grace of God.

We, too, are touched by God's grace. Look around you and see all that God has given you. Think about your family and friends. Think of how in times of trouble your family and friends were there for you to help you over the hurdles of life. Make this your starting point. Make it the place where you begin to build a life of prayer and openness to the Lord—a place where you will receive the Living Water.

How deep is your well?

Our Lord is the Living Water who resides in the well of our souls. The stronger our faith and the deeper the well, the more refreshed our souls will be!

PRAYER

May the Living Water who resides in my soul bring me refreshment and enrich my spiritual life.

Offer one Our Father, One Hail Mary, and one Glory Be.

2.

$\mathcal{P}$ADRE PIO'S EARLY LIFE AND VISITATIONS

You want to know when Jesus began to favor his poor
creature with heavenly visions. If I am not mistaken
these must have begun not long after the novitiate.
—Padre Pio

On January 6, 1903, Francesco Forgione, age fifteen, entered the novitiate of the Capuchin Franciscans in Morcone, Italy. Not long after that, the heavenly visions began in earnest.

We know very little about the early life of Francesco. His parents didn't keep records or diaries that we know about. What we do know we learned from Padre Pio's spiritual directors and friends, but it is barely enough to put together a biography.

Francesco Forgione was born in Pietrelcina, Italy, on May 25, 1887, to Grazio Forgione and Maria Giuseppa (Peppa) Di Nunzio. The following day, he was baptized in the Church of Sant'Anna. In a letter to Maria Campanile, in 1922, Padre Pio wrote: "The Lord from my birth showed me signs of a very special predilection."[1]

And so it seems the heavenly visits started at an early age. Padre Agostino tells us, "Francesco was barely five years old when he began to experience the first ecstasies and apparitions." At the time, young Francesco said little about what was happening—in his letters, he once recalled sitting with his mother on a bench when Jesus came to play with him. He didn't say anything to his mother at the time—he thought Jesus and Our Lady talked that way with everyone![2]

Once that door to the invisible world was opened for him, the ecstasies and apparitions were not the only thing that Francesco experienced. There were also demonic apparitions, and the demons would forever taunt him. If Francesco had not been given special graces, he would not have been able to cope with these encounters.

Padre Pio told Fr. Caccioppoli, "When I was in the crib, and my mom extinguished the lamp, I saw those horrible monsters and screamed, terrified. Then mom turned the lamp back on, and the monsters disappeared, and I stopped screaming."[3] He also told Fr. Caccioppoli of the visible companionship of his guardian angel, who had been with him since infancy. God never left young Francesco to fight the demons alone.

Has there ever been a time when you felt you had a glimpse of the invisible world—your guardian angel, who is entrusted to you from the moment you were conceived in the womb? Perhaps you have never seen your angel with your eyes—most people don't. But you can be sure that when you are in need of protection, your angel stands ready to guard and guide you.

PREPARING FOR HIS VOCATION

At the age of six, Francesco was sent to graze sheep with an older boy, Ubaldo Vecchiarino, who everyone called Baldino. Seeing young Francesco praying out in the fields, the older boy commented to his friend, "You, when you pray, you seem to be dead, that you are no more on this earth."[4]

Aside from a few memories from neighbors, Francesco passed his early years virtually unnoticed except that, in the village, he was known to all for his exemplary conduct and his attendance morning and evening at the parish church. Francesco and Baldino went to private school together in the evening in the home of Cosimo Scocca. Baldino said, "Francesco was the only one to answer the teacher's questions."[5]

In September 1898, after expressing a desire to become a priest and in order to meet the requirements of the monastery, Francesco began private lessons with Domenico Tizzani. The tuition for the lessons was five lire per month. That was a great deal of money for the Forgione family. After a few months with Don Tizzani, Francesco went to study with Angelo Caccavo. Francesco got his elementary diploma while studying with Mr. Caccavo.

His parents seemed to recognize God's call upon Francesco and did what they could to help him get the education he needed to answer that call. To earn the money required to pay for Francesco's studies, Grazio Forgione went to work in Brazil in 1897. However, he could find very little employment there and came back to Italy without money.

In 1899, Forgione traveled to America where, through the help of a cousin, he found work as a farm laborer in Mahoningtown, near New Castle, Pennsylvania. By staying with his cousin, he was able to send money home every week and pay for Francesco's private tutors. Padre Pio later recalled, "My father crossed the ocean twice to give me the possibility to become a friar."[6]

Can you think of a time when you had a desire to do something and needed the support of other people to help you achieve your goal? Even when our desire is inspired by God, we will sometimes experience opposition and hardship. In the struggle, we learn the virtue of perseverance—as we discover through the life of Padre Pio.

PADRE PIO'S CALL TO THE PRIESTHOOD

At the time of Francesco's First Communion and Confirmation on September 27, 1899, at the age of twelve, a beautiful revelation began. The first inward thoughts of a religious life began to bloom. In a 1914 letter to Padre Agostino, Padre Pio recalls his Confirmation:

Pietrelcina, May 14, 1914

My very dear father,

May Jesus and Mary always be in your heart and make you holy.

In the last few days, we have had the holy visit of the Archbishop, his grace, Monsignor Bonacci, he also administered confirmation to about 450 people. . . .

I have never assisted at such a holy ceremony since the day I was confirmed. I cried with consolation during the sacred ceremony, which reminded me of what the Holy Spirit, the Paraclete, made me feel on the day when I myself received the Sacrament of Confirmation, a most unique day for me and unforgettable for my whole life. How tenderly was I moved that day by this consoling Spirit! At the thought of it, I feel myself burning all over with the most ardent flame which burns and consumes me but causes me no pain.

How happy I would be to be consumed as soon as possible by this flame! Oh, yes!

The merciful Father of Jesus reveals in the end his presence to those who seek him ardently, and since no one can see him without dying, let me [die], and I shall consider myself most happy, for the gain by far surpasses the loss.

My soul is filled with the impatient longing to see yourself itself possessed, once and for all, by this great God, whose love has stolen and pierced my heart. . . .

Fra Pio[7]

A short time after Francesco's Confirmation, he began to feel a calling to a religious order. On October 5, 1901, at age fourteen, Francesco sent a letter to his father in America and told him that he had a desire to become a Capuchin priest. At fifteen, he received an inner warning of the implacable struggles he would have to endure with the devil, and in point of fact he would have to face up to Satan. The path he chose to follow was enlightened by divine grace.

Overcoming all the difficulties placed before him, Francesco was clothed in the habit of the Capuchins on January 22, 1903. He was given the name Fra Pio of Pietrelcina. On January 22, 1904, he made his first profession of the vows of poverty, chastity, and obedience, and four years later, according to canonical law, he pronounced his solemn vows "for the one and only purpose," as he wrote himself in the official document, "of attending to the good of my soul and devoting myself entirely to God's service."[8]

REFLECTION

From the moment of his birth, Francesco walked in the footsteps of the Lord. As children we need our parents to tell us about God and teach us good values. Padre Pio seemed to possess those values from his earliest years. The fact that he chose to go to church and pray instead of playing tells us that early on he was filled with the Holy Spirit. His parents reinforced those graces and encouraged him to cooperate with them.

The most important thing that parents can give their children is religious beliefs. These beliefs open the path for higher values. How did your parents lead you along the path to paradise? If you have children (or hope to have them one day), how do you intend to lead your children along this heavenly path? We must teach our children to be faithful, to love the Lord and place everything in God's hands.

How deep is your well?

PRAYER

May the Living Water who resides in my soul bring me refreshment and enrich my spiritual life.

Offer one Our Father, one Hail Mary, and one Glory Be.

3.

$\mathcal{T}$HE SPIRITUAL GIFTS REVEALED

You know, they are a mystery to me, too.

—Padre Pio

Padre Pio was an extraordinary man with many extraordinary spiritual gifts. Those closest to him attest to seeing those gifts made manifest not only after the appearance of the stigmata, but long before that—when he first entered the seminary. These events were recorded under sealed testimony by Padre Pio's superiors, and some of these events were not revealed until after his death, during the investigation for his cause for sainthood.

Among the spiritual and mystical charisms attributed to Padre Pio before and after he received the stigmata on September 20, 1918, are the gifts of healing, bilocation, levitation, prophecy, miracles, extraordinary abstinence from both sleep and nourishment, the ability to read hearts, the gift of tongues, the gift of conversions, the gift of tears, and the fragrance of holiness (the fragrance from his wounds).

Are you familiar with the extraordinary spiritual gifts or charisms that God gives to some for service in the Church?

You can read about them in 1 Corinthians 12:1–11.[1] *Unlike the gifts of the Holy Spirit that we all receive at baptism, these supernatural gifts of the Holy Spirit are intended to aid those who are chosen by God to serve his Church in a special way. The stories of various saints, like Padre Pio, show us how these gifts are given to enrich the lives of others and lead us on a path to holiness.*

THE BILOCATING PRIEST

The first recorded bilocation of Padre Pio took place on January 18, 1905, when Pio was a young monk. Bilocation is a state in which a person occupies two places at the same time. In this case, Padre Pio was in the choir loft of the monastery of Sant'Elia a Pianisi and also in the garden of the Rizzani family in Udine, Italy.

Padre Pio's account of this event, which he gave to his superiors, was unsealed at the time of his cause for beatification and presented to the Archiepiscopal Curia of Manfredonia. When the curia compared his testimony to that of Giovanna Rizzani, who was born on the evening of January 18, 1905, the similarity of the facts was unmistakable.

On the evening she went into labor, Giovanna's mother saw a young monk walking in the garden; later, the mother told her daughter, he witnessed the birth of Giovanna. The document written by Padre Pio was never read by Giovanna Rizzani, and Padre Pio's bilocation on that evening was known only to his superiors. It wasn't revealed until this document was unsealed.

So, we can see that even as a young brother, Padre Pio already began to experience these spiritual gifts. We cannot explain how Padre Pio had such gifts; in fact, Padre Pio had no explanation himself. Once he was asked about his gifts, and he replied, "You know, they are a mystery to me, too." Above all, Padre Pio never felt worthy of these gifts. He always remained humble.

WHY DOES GOD GIVE SPECIAL CHARISMS?

As Catholics, we believe that we receive the Holy Spirit in the Sacraments of Baptism and Confirmation. The Holy Spirit endows us with certain gifts, which continue to bear fruit throughout our lives as we cooperate with them: wisdom, understanding, counsel, fortitude, knowledge, piety, and fear of the Lord. And yet some of us—including Padre Pio—receive additional gifts that enable us to serve the Church more fully. We read about these supernatural gifts in 1 Corinthians:

> To one is given through the Spirit the expression of wisdom; to another the expression of knowledge according to the same Spirit; to another faith by the same Spirit; to another gifts of healing by the one Spirit; to another mighty deeds; to another prophecy; to another discernment of spirits; to another varieties of tongues; to another interpretation of tongues. But

one and the same Spirit produces all of these, distrib-
uting them individually to each person as he wishes.
(1 Cor 12:8–11)

To whom does the Holy Spirit give these gifts? St. Paul
tells us that, too: "Some people God has designated in the
church to be, first, apostles; second, prophets; third, teachers; then, mighty deeds; then, gifts of healing, assistance,
administration, and varieties of tongues" (v. 28). Because
he served the people of God in so many special ways—as
priest, healer, confessor, and intercessor—and because
of the intimate relationship he maintained with the Lord
throughout his life, Padre Pio was entrusted with many
extraordinary gifts in order to fulfill his mission.

More Spiritual Gifts

Let's take a look at some of the other spiritual gifts Padre
Pio received. These gifts—like the stigmata and other gifts
not listed here—remained with him throughout his life.

Nourishment through the Eucharist alone. Like many
saints, Padre Pio was empowered by grace. He routinely
denied himself both sleep and food without ill effects and
was wholly nourished by the Eucharist. Padre Agostino
recorded one instance while Padre Pio was residing at the
monastery of Venafro. He subsisted for at least twenty
days on only the Eucharist without taking any other
nourishment.

The gift of tears. Think about a tender moment in your life—the love you felt on your wedding day, at the birth of your child, at your child's marriage or profession of religious vows. If you have experienced any of these things, you will understand what I am talking about. The love Padre Pio had for the Lord was that kind of love, and it was a love he felt constantly.

This tender love that we feel may cause us to cry tears of joy at special moments in our lives. We have no control over these tears. For us, these moments are few and far between, but for Padre Pio these moments came often. The love he felt for the Lord caused him to cry constantly. This was one of Padre Pio's spiritual gifts.

Padre Pio cried frequently and abundantly. Br. Leo (Fra Leone), a classmate of Padre Pio from 1903 to 1908, testified to this fact: "While praying, Padre Pio was always crying, silently, and so abundantly that his tears were leaving traces on the stone pavement of the choir. As youngsters, we made fun of him. So, he took the habit of lying on the floor with a large handkerchief in front of him. After praying he would take the handkerchief that was all wet. You could have squeezed it!"[2]

Visions of the invisible world. Of all the tasks entrusted to him, by far the most challenging and exhausting for the humble Capuchin was that of spiritual warfare. From the time he was fifteen years old, Padre Pio was actively resisting the forces of evil and declaring the power of God to bring healing and restoration. From the time he first entered the monastery he understood that this would be his responsibility, for he received a vision that would change his life forever. The following is testimony to the event that he gave to his superiors, taken from Padre Pio's autobiographical notes:

In the name of Jesus. Amen.

Everything which I am about to relate . . . is set down in virtue of holy obedience. God alone can fully understand the great repugnance with which I write these things. He alone is my witness, and if he had not greatly strengthened me in the respect due to authority, I should have resolutely refused to the point of rebellion and should never have been induced to set down what I am about to write, fully aware as I am of the wickedness of this soul which was favored by heaven with such singular graces. May God be pleased to help and strengthen me, so that I may overcome the confusion I feel in manifesting what I'm about to relate.

Here is the first extraordinary call to this soul, in order that he should leave the world and the path to his own damnation and devote himself entirely to God's service.

This soul had felt strongly, from his earliest years, the vocation to the religious state, but as he grew older, alas, he began to drink great draughts of this world's vanity. In the heart of this poor creature a powerful battle began between the increasingly strong vocation, on the one hand, and a sweet but false delight of the things of the world on the other. Without a doubt, with the passage of time the feelings would have triumph over the spirit and would have smothered the good seed of the divine call. But the Lord, who desired this soul for himself, was pleased to favor this person with the vision I am about to describe.

While he was meditating one day on his vocation and wondering how he could make up his mind to bid farewell to the world in order to devote himself entirely to God in a holy enclosure, his senses were suddenly suspended, and he was made to gaze with the eyes of his intellect on things quite different from those seen by the bodily eyes.

He beheld at his side a majestic figure of rare beauty, radiant as the sun. This man took him by the hand, and he heard him say: "Come with me, for it is fitting that you fight as a valiant warrior." He led him to a vast plain, where there was a great multitude of people, divided into two groups. On one side he saw men of beautiful countenance, clad in snow-white garments; on the other, in the second group, were black-robed men of hideous appearance who seemed like dark shadows.

Between these two large groups was a wide space in which that soul was placed by his guide. As he gazed intently at the two groups, suddenly, in the middle of that space which separated them, a man advanced, so tall that his forehead touched the clouds, while his countenance was that of a hideous black monster.

At this sight the poor soul was completely disconcerted, and he felt his life suspended. The strange figure advanced nearer and the guide at the side of that soul informed him that he would have to fight this individual. At these words the poor thing turned pale, trembled all over and was on the point of falling to the ground in a faint, so great was the terror he experienced.

The guide supported him with one arm until he had recovered somewhat from the fright. The soul then turned to his guide and begged him to save him from the fury of that strange being, because, he told him, that man was so strong that the strength of all men combined would not be sufficient to knock him down.

[The guide replied,] "All resistance is useless; it is advisable that you fight this man. Take heart; enter confidently into combat, go forward courageously, for I shall be close to you. I will assist you and not allow him to overcome you. In reward for your victory over him, I'll give you a splendid crown to adorn your head."

The poor soul took heart and entered into the combat with that dreadful and mysterious being. The impact was tremendous, but with the aid of his guide who never left his side, he finally overcame his adversary, threw him to the ground, and obliged him to flee.

Then the guide, faithful to his promise, took from beneath his robes a crown of exceptional splendor, of indescribable beauty, which he put on his head. But after an instant he withdrew the crown, saying as he did so: "I shall reserve for you an even more beautiful crown if you succeed in combat with that being with whom you have already fought. He will return continually to the attack to regain his lost honor: Fight valiantly and have no doubt about my assistance. Keep your eyes wide open, for that mysterious being will endeavor to take you by surprise. Don't be afraid of his attacks or his dreadful aspects. Remember what I have promised you: that I'll always be close to you and help you so that you'll always succeed in overcoming him."

When that mysterious being had been vanquished, the entire multitude of hideous men took flight with shrieks and imprecations and deafening cries, while from the other . . . came the sound of applause and praise for the splendid man more radiant than the sun who had assisted the poor soul so magnificently in the fierce combat. Here the vision ended.

This vision filled that poor soul with such great courage that it seemed like a thousand years before he was able to abandon the world forever, to devote himself entirely to God's service in a religious institute.

The vision just described was understood by that soul, although not quite clearly. The Lord, however, was pleased to manifest the meaning of this symbolic vision to him by a further one a few days before he entered religion. I say a few days before, because he had already applied to the Provincial Superior for admission and had received an affirmative reply, when the Lord granted him this further vision which was purely intellectual.

This occurred on the Feast of the Lord's Circumcision, five days before leaving his home. He had received Holy Communion and was engaged in intimate converse with the Lord when his soul was suddenly flooded with supernatural light. By means of this most pure light he understood in a flash that his entry into religion in the service of the heavenly King meant being exposed to combat with that mysterious being from hell with whom he had fought in the previous vision.

He then understood, and that was sufficient to hearten him, that although the demons would be present at battles to make fun of his failures, on the other hand there was nothing to fear, because the angels would also be there to applaud his victories over Satan. Both were symbolized by the two groups he had seen in the previous view. He also understood that although the enemy he had to fight was a terrible one, he had no reason to be afraid, because Jesus Christ himself, represented by that radiant person who had acted as his guide, would assist him, would always be at his side to help him and he would reward him in paradise for his victories achieved, provided he placed his trust in him alone and fought generously.

The vision made that soul strong and generous in bidding farewell to the world. However, it must not be imagined that he had nothing to suffer in the lower part of his soul as he abandoned his own family to whom he was strongly attached. He felt even his bones being crushed as this leave-taking approached and the pain was so intense that he almost fainted.

As the day of his departure drew nearer, the anguish increased. On the last night he spent with his family, the Lord came to console him by yet another vision. He beheld in all their majesty, Jesus and his Blessed Mother who encouraged him and assured him of their predilection. Finally, Jesus placed a hand on his head and this was sufficient to strengthen the higher part of his soul, so that he shed not a single tear at this painful leave-taking, although at that moment he was suffering agonies in soul and body.[3]

As a reward for taking on the battle against evil, the Lord bestowed special graces on Padre Pio so that he would receive solace in the moments of those attacks by the devil.

At times, as you will notice in the above description and in his letters, Padre Pio refers to himself in third person (he), especially when he is writing about an event. However, when he is speaking about the event to his spiritual director, he uses the first person (I). It's as if the person who is affected, who is a part of the event (he), is not himself but is in fact the person who left this world to defend the Lord against Satan.

ℛEFLECTION

What do you think of this account of the spiritual warfare to which Padre Pio was called? Have you ever known anyone who was called by God to intercede in this way?

Most of us will never enter directly into combat with demonic forces, like Padre Pio. And yet each of us is expected to resist evil and to uphold goodness in our corner of the world. How have you felt called to do this?

In some parts of the world, it is impossible to resist evil without personal risk. That, too, is a gift—the gift of martyrdom. There have been moments in my life when I have wondered what would happen if the Lord asked me to lay down my life for him. Would I be like Padre Pio and say yes? I like to think so.

How deep is your well?

℘RAYER

May the Living Water who resides in my soul bring me refreshment and enrich my spiritual life.

Offer one Our Father, one Hail Mary, and one Glory Be.

4.

$\mathcal{M}$YSTICAL TOUCHES

The heart of Jesus and my own, allow me to use the
expression, were fused. No longer were two hearts
beating but only one. My own heart had disappeared,
as a drop of water is lost in the ocean.

—Padre Pio

On July 6, 1910, Padre Pio began to experience severe
pains in his chest, starting in his lungs. Because his superiors feared that he might die, they decided to ordain him to
the priesthood nine months before the scheduled date of
his ordination, while he was still underage. This decision
to forgo the minimum age for ordination coincided with
the appearance of Padre Pio's first visible stigmata.

We begin with a letter from Fra Pio to Padre Benedetto Nardella, his superior and spiritual director:

Pietrelcina, July 6, 1910

My dear Father,
    For several days I have been tormented by a fresh
pain at the base of my left lung. Perhaps Jesus will
really have done with me this time. This new pain is

more severe than any of the others. It makes me almost powerless to do anything and at times I can hardly speak.

Every day . . . a fresh cloud has come to darken the horizon of my soul. The Prince of Darkness is starting a new war against me. Since he was defeated by my obedience to you . . . he has started another, no less furious battle against me. After the numerically innumerable temptations to which I am subject day by day, a doubt which is capable of throwing my mind into confusion still remains.

. . . My pen is powerless to describe what goes on in my soul at these moments of concealment. More than ever when I approach Holy Communion, the malignant enemy makes me feel uncertain as to whether or not I have dismissed this temptation.

Yours,
Fra Pio[1]

Padre Pio passed through many dark nights. He questioned everything and everyone around him. There was no relief from the torments of the devil. The closer he came to God, the fiercer the attack. The devil was relentless!

On August 10, 1910, Fra Pio was ordained Padre Pio. A few weeks later, on September 7, while Padre Pio was praying in Piana Romana near his family's home, Jesus and the Virgin Mary appeared to him. It was on this occasion that Jesus gave Padre Pio the visible stigmata. As a child, Francesco used to go to Piana Romana to pray in the shade of a straw hut built under an elm tree. Today the straw hut is a chapel, a stump of the elm preserved inside it.

Fr. Salvatore Pannullo, pastor of the parish church in Pietrelcina, gave the following testimony about the afternoon of September 7, 1910, when Padre Pio showed him the wounds of the stigmata. Padre Pio said: "Father, do me a favor. Ask Jesus to take them away. I want to suffer, to die from suffering, but in secret."[2]

The two priests prayed together, and God answered their prayers. The wounds disappeared, but the suffering continued. These were the invisible stigmata of Padre Pio. When Fr. Pannullo was told in 1918 that the wounds had appeared on Padre Pio, he replied, "You see them now. I saw them in 1910."[3]

HOW DID PADRE PIO ENDURE SUCH SUFFERING?

When I decided to write this book, one of the first things I came upon in my research was the "fusion of hearts," a uniting of the heart of Jesus with the heart of Padre Pio. This fusion of hearts was a prelude to the transverberation (piercing of the heart) and visible stigmata of Padre Pio. All these are considered his "mystical touches."

Until I read about the mystical touches, I did not understand how Padre Pio could bear the pain and agony he experienced each day. These mystical touches caused Padre Pio to feel like he would die for love of the Lord, and it was this love that helped him endure all the pain and suffering. Through these mystical touches, the Lord began to prepare Padre Pio for the sword that would pierce his heart and remain with him until his death.

What are mystical touches? They are delightful feelings supernaturally imprinted by God through a spiritual contact "on the base or point of the soul," on the "apex of the spirit."[4] Alternately referred to in the *Letters* as a "fusion of hearts," "a substantial touch," and "a kiss of love," these mystical touches can involve varying degrees of intensity.

In the following excerpt from the *Letters*, Padre Pio explains to Padre Agostino what happened to him on the evening of April 16, 1912, the night that his heart fused with the heart of the Lord:

> When Mass was over, I remained with Jesus in thanksgiving. Oh, how sweet was the colloquy with paradise that morning. It was such that, although I want to tell you all about it, I cannot. There were things which cannot be translated into human language without losing their deep and heavenly meaning. The heart of Jesus and my own, allow me to use the expression, were fused. No longer were two hearts beating but only

one. My own heart had disappeared, as a drop of water is lost in the ocean. Jesus was its paradise, its king. My joy was so intense and deep that I could bear no more, and tears of happiness poured down my cheeks.[5]

In excerpts from the following letters, we hear about the substantial touch and kiss of love.

Father, may I be allowed to express myself freely at least to you: I am crucified by love! I can no longer go on. This is too delicate a food for one accustomed to coarse fare and it is for this reason that it continually causes me extreme spiritual indigestion, to the point at which my poor soul cries out in acute pain and love at the same time. My wretched soul cannot adapt to this new manner of the Lord's dealings with it. Thus, the kiss and the touch, which I would describe as substantial, that this most loving heavenly Father imprints on my soul still causes me extreme suffering. (May 18, 1915)[6]

Only once did I feel in the deepest recesses of my spirit something so delicate that I do not know how to explain it to you. First of all, without seeing anything, my soul became aware of His presence and then, as I would describe it, He came so close to my soul that I felt His touch. To give you a feeble image of it, it was like what happens when your body feels the pressure of another body against it.

I don't know how to describe it otherwise, I merely confess that I was seized with the greatest fear in the beginning and that, by degrees, this fear became a heavenly rapture. It seemed to me that I was no longer in the state of a traveler, and I cannot tell you whether or not at that moment I was still aware of being in this body of mine. Only God knows this, and I am unable to tell you anything further to give you a better idea of this event. (August 3, 1916)[7]

Here is what happened to me on that day [the Feast of Corpus Christi, May 30, 1918]. During my Mass in the morning, I was touched by a living breath. I cannot convey the slightest idea of what happened within me in that fleeting moment. I felt completely shaken, filled with extreme terror and I almost passed away. This was followed by a state of total calm such that I have never felt before. . . . This terror, agitation and calm in quick succession were not caused by the sight of anything but by something which I felt touching me in the deepest recesses of my soul. I am unable to say any more about this occurrence. May God be pleased to make you understand what really happened to me. (July 27, 1918)[8]

In these letters to his spiritual directors, we hear Padre Pio express fear of what is happening to him. He wants to believe these touches are good, but he is afraid that they may be something else; perhaps it's the devil trying to deceive him. Padre Pio is shaken by these experiences and perhaps momentarily tries to escape them. But he comes to recognize these occurrences as mystical touches, which the Lord gives to him to strengthen his soul and prepare him for the battles he will face.

Padre Pio's faith in the Lord brought him through every crisis. He loved the Lord so much that he analyzed every feeling, every sensation, every touch. It was his desire to protect the Lord from all enemies, and he did this by questioning everything. Only after he was truly convinced that the Lord was sending him these mystical touches did he accept them and treasure them.

REFLECTION

Do you recognize the Lord in your life? You may not receive mystical touches, but you do receive signs and blessings from the Lord every day. When you are faced with choices, how do you make the right decision? Do you weigh your thoughts? Do you try to choose what is healthy and good—physically, spiritually, and emotionally—rather than just accepting whatever comes along? Do you ask yourself if your thoughts, words, and deeds are pleasing to the Lord?

How deep is your well?

It's difficult for us to imagine what it would be like for the Lord to breathe on us or touch our souls in such a deep and profound way as he touched Padre Pio—who felt he would die from the experience. And yet, the Lord does touch us in many ways every day.

With faith we can overcome any obstacle. When you find yourself on the brink of committing a sin, pray and ask the Lord for his help, then take a step back from the situation and think. Feel the calm that comes from the Lord answering our prayers, a feeling that everything will be all right. Recognize the Lord's touch in that moment. Draw deep from that well of faith, and choose what is right and what will please him.

How deep is your well?

PRAYER

May the Living Water who resides in my soul bring me refreshment and enrich my spiritual life.

Offer one Our Father, one Hail Mary, and one Glory Be.

5.

$\mathcal{W}$INDS OF CHANGE

The vision disappeared and I became aware that my hands, feet and side were dripping blood. Imagine the agony I experienced and continue to experience almost every day. The heart wound bleeds continually, especially from Thursday evening until Saturday.

—Padre Pio

In the early months of 1919, news began to spread about the friar who lived on Mount Gargano. Rumors of Padre Pio's stigmata could be heard everywhere. Beginning in March 1919, crowds began to cause disturbances in and around the Capuchin friary as groups of people arrived from the surrounding towns.

By June, the first special news correspondents arrived, anxious to get the incredible story for their newspapers. Padre Pio had become a big news item; hundreds of thousands of people were seeking out the humble friar for the sole purpose of confessing their sins. Imagine how demanding this must have been, to meet the pastoral needs of all these people! This intense pastoral activity is reflected in Padre Pio's letters. At times he could barely take his pen in hand until midnight. Padre Pio admitted that he was "worn out by the overabundance of work performed all day long . . . I now have to work for nineteen hours without a break."[1]

Lucia Fiorentino, one of Padre Pio's first spiritual daughters, writes in her autobiography, "The crowd exceeded all limits. It came to the point where it was no longer possible to see Padre Pio or receive a word from him. I myself remained in greatest desolation for two months."[2]

In addition to spending so many hours in the confessional, Padre Pio received piles of mail from all over the world. He would stay up until early in the morning answering his correspondence. These letters were important to Padre Pio because he felt a strong obligation to the people who had placed themselves under his spiritual care and guidance.

All this public attention can be traced back to the reappearance of Padre Pio's visible stigmata, which occurred on September 20, 1918. Let's go back and see how this all came to be.

A Celestial Messenger

On August 5, 1918, while hearing the confession of one of the seminarians at the monastery, Padre Pio received a strange celestial messenger. He described the vision in this manner in a letter to Padre Benedetto on August 21:

[As I was hearing the boy's confession,] I was suddenly terrorized by the sight of a celestial person who presented himself to my mind's eye. He had in his hand a sort of weapon like a very long sharp-pointed steel blade which seemed to emit fire. At the very instant that I saw all this, I saw that person hurl the weapon into my soul with all his might. I cried out with difficulty and felt I was dying. I asked the boy to leave because I felt ill and no longer had the strength to continue. This agony lasted uninterruptedly until the morning of the 7th.

I cannot tell you how much I suffered during this period of anguish. Even my entrails were torn and ruptured by the weapon, and nothing was spared. From that day on I have been mortally wounded. I feel in the depths of my soul a wound that is always open, and which causes me continual agony.[3]

Who was this celestial being, and why did he pierce Padre Pio with this sharp-pointed sword? What Padre Pio described was the act of transverberation—being pierced through the heart by an angel of God. The Latin term means "to pierce all the way through." The heart has pangs that are both physical and mystical. This was the prelude to the reoccurrence of the visible stigmata.

By September 20, 1918, the pains of the transverberation had ceased, and Padre Pio was in "profound peace." On that day, as he was praying in the choir loft of the Church of Santa Maria delle Grazie, a similar being appeared again, and Padre Pio had another experience of religious ecstasy. When the ecstasy ended, Padre Pio had received the visible stigmata, the five wounds of Christ Crucified.

In a letter to Padre Benedetto dated October 22, 1918, Padre Pio describes his experience of receiving the visible stigmata:

> On the morning of the 20th of last month, in the choir, after I had celebrated Mass, I yielded to a drowsiness similar to a sweet sleep. I saw before me a mysterious person similar to the one I had seen on the evening of August 5th. The only difference was that his hands and feet and side were dripping blood. This sight terrified me and what I felt at that moment is indescribable. I thought I should have died if the Lord had not intervened and strengthened my heart which was about to burst out of my chest. The vision disappeared and I became aware that my hands, feet and side were dripping blood. Imagine the agony I experienced and continue to experience almost every day. The heart wound bleeds continually, especially from Thursday evening until Saturday.
>
> Dear Father, I am dying of pain because of the wounds and the resulting embarrassment I feel deep in my soul. I am afraid I shall bleed to death if the Lord does not hear my heartfelt supplication to relieve me of this condition. Will Jesus, who is so good, grant me

this grace? Will he at least free me from the embarrassment caused by these outward signs? I will raise my voice and will not stop imploring him until in his mercy he takes away, not the wound or the pain, which is impossible since I wish to be inebriated with pain, but these outward signs which cause me such embarrassment and unbearable humiliation.[4]

THE HIGHS AND LOWS OF LOVE

The letters written by Padre Pio to his superiors during this period are rich in details about the mystical phenomena. Padre Pio talks of love and pain as a "twofold love, vertical toward God and horizontal toward others,"[5] as his following statements bear witness:

- "I am consumed by love of God and love of my neighbor."[6]
- "I feel I am drowned in the immense ocean of the love of my Beloved."[7]
- "God is always fixed in my mind and imprinted on my heart. Equally striking are the expressions which reveal the horizontal dimension of the love that consumed him."[8]
- "I am carried away by an overwhelming desire to live for others."[9]
- "I have worked, I want to work. I have prayed, I want to pray; I have wept and I want to weep always for my brothers in exile."[10]

This time seems to be marked by a continual sense of spiritual delight followed by immense spiritual desolation. Many times, Padre Pio seems to be passing through a kind of dark night, where his soul goes forth in a painful fog and he believes that none of his actions are pleasing to God. Rather, he has an almost certain conviction that he is offending God, and everything tortures him and causes him to suffer agony. Padre Pio said, "It is an obsession which runs my heart and pierces my brain."[11]

And yet it is clear from the uproar of the disorderly crowds who flocked to San Giovanni Rotondo and the intense and constant pastoral activity required of Padre Pio that the people around him, who had just endured World War I, looked to him as a consoling symbol of hope as they rebuilt their lives. At this time, those close to Padre Pio became aware that there were other extraordinary events surrounding him—which will become the focus of the next chapter.

ℛEFLECTION

As I write this, it is Holy Thursday and I have just come home from the Mass of the Last Supper. After Mass we had Eucharistic Adoration, and I sat for some time reflecting on the Passion of Christ. Reading through my little prayer book of the Stations of the Cross, I thought about why the Lord gave his life for us. Without a doubt it was for love. Everything he did, the suffering, his death, he did it all for love of us!

What does the Lord teach us through the Stations of the Cross? He teaches us that we should share his Cross because when we have crosses in our lives, he shares them with us. He teaches us that the Cross isn't the end; it is the beginning. It is a part of the road that we must journey on in life. Life would not be complete without crosses. What's important is not how many crosses we carry; no, it's how many times the Lord will stand beside us and carry us and our crosses to the end of the journey. Jesus died on the Cross so we might live!

The roadway to heaven is lined with crosses. Will you gladly journey on this road and raise your cross high for love of the Lord? In your most difficult times, will you willingly place everything in his hands?

How deep is your well?

Think again of Padre Pio and the cross he carried. Though he would have preferred to suffer in secret, by early 1919, the news about his stigmata had spread far and wide. In a unique way, by God's grace Padre Pio embodied the teaching of St. Paul to the Romans: "Put on the Lord Jesus Christ, and make no provision for the desires of the flesh" (13:14). Most of us will not do this in a literal sense, as Padre Pio did. Yet we are all called to pursue Christ and embrace lives of virtue and discipline out of love for Christ. What form does this take in your life?

How deep is your well?

What we see in Padre Pio is a man who, like Jesus, gladly suffered for love. Padre Pio loved no one in life more than Jesus. On many occasions Padre Pio asked the Lord to take him—not because he didn't want to suffer. No, he gladly suffered for the Lord. He wanted the Lord to take him because he couldn't bear to live without the Lord. His love of the Lord was all-consuming. Padre Pio couldn't imagine living one moment of his life without the Lord at his side. This love caused Padre Pio to constantly cry for the Lord.

Can you imagine feeling this way? *How deep is your well?*

Prayer

Have you prayed the Stations of the Cross in your parish? This devotion isn't just for Lent—we can pray the fourteen Stations anytime and anywhere. The fourteen images of Christ's Passion and Death are lasting images. We can use our mind's eye to make the Stations of the Cross at home or when walking or driving. How many of the Stations can you name (without peeking)?

- Jesus is condemned to death.
- Jesus takes up his Cross.
- Jesus falls the first time.
- Jesus meets his mother.
- Simon of Cyrene helps Jesus bear his Cross.
- Veronica wipes the face of Jesus.
- Jesus falls a second time.
- Jesus meets the women of Jerusalem.
- Jesus falls a third time.
- Jesus is stripped of his clothes.
- Jesus is nailed to the Cross.
- Jesus dies on the Cross.
- Jesus is taken down from the Cross.
- Jesus is laid in the tomb.

Make the Stations a part of your daily prayers. Help Jesus to carry his Cross every day, and when the day comes that you need help carrying your cross, be assured that the Lord will be standing beside you to help you. As we close, let's say this little prayer:

May the Living Water who resides in my soul bring me refreshment and enrich my spiritual life.

Offer one Our Father, one Hail Mary, and one Glory Be.

6.

ƒIVE MILLION CONFESSIONS

There have been periods when I heard confessions without interruption for eighteen hours consecutively. I don't have a moment to myself. But God helps me effectively in my ministry. I feel the strength to renounce everything, so long as souls return to Jesus and love Jesus.

—Padre Pio

Padre Pio regularly spent up to fifteen hours a day in the confessional. In a letter to Padre Benedetto on June 3, 1919, nine months after receiving the stigmata, Padre Pio wrote:

My very dear Father,

May Jesus bless and comfort you.

I haven't a free moment. All my time is spent in setting my brothers free from the snares of Satan. May God be blessed. Please don't afflict me further like the others by appealing to charity because the greatest charity is that of snatching souls from Satan so as to win them for Christ. This is precisely what I am doing constantly by day and night.

I don't think any doctor has come here from Bar-letta. Innumerable people of all classes and both sexes come here for the sole purpose of making their confession and I am only sought for this purpose. There are some wonderful conversions.

Let everyone be satisfied, therefore, with a simple remembrance as I constantly remember them all in Jesus' presence.

I kiss your hand and ask your holy blessing.

Fra Pio, Capuchin[1]

In the Confessional

As I was researching material for this book, I came across a wonderful article by Br. Michael Dimond called "Confessions with Padre Pio," which shared fascinating details about Padre Pio as a confessor.[2] Did you know . . .

- It is estimated that Padre Pio heard a total of five million confessions in his lifetime. From 1918 to 1923, Padre Pio heard confessions fifteen to nineteen hours a day. In the 1940s and 1950s, he generally heard confessions for five to eight hours a day. The average time a person spent in the confessional with Padre Pio was three minutes.[3]

- Beginning in January 1950, so many people wanted their confession heard by Padre Pio that it became necessary to open a ticket office and hand out numbers. People waited for two to three weeks for their confession to be heard. Once your confession was heard, you had to wait eight days before receiving the Sacrament of Penance from Padre Pio again.[4]

- The one thing that Padre Pio demanded of each penitent was honesty, each confession a true conversion. If the penitent wasn't honest or firm in his resolve, Padre Pio would say, "Get out." Sometimes he would snap shut the panel in their face.[5] It was essential that each penitent be sorrowful for their sins and resolve to not sin again.

- Padre Pio even threw priests and bishops out of his confessional. He once told a priest: "If you knew fully what a fearful thing it is to sit in the tribunal of the confessional! We are administering the Blood of Christ. We must be careful that we do not fling it about by being too easy-going or negligent."[6]

When was the last time you went to confession? Is it time to go again and make a fresh start in your life? Ask Padre Pio to pray for you for the courage to follow through. Jesus is waiting for you.

TESTIMONIES OF CONVERSION

The following are the testimonies of people who went to Padre Pio for the Sacrament of Reconciliation (Confession).

Andre Mandato, the husband of Padre Pio biographer Graziella DeNunzio Mandato, spoke about the time he went to confession to Padre Pio:

I had been going to church every Sunday, but I had no strong belief in confession. I went very seldom. I started to believe in confession only after I went to Padre Pio. The first time I confessed to him, he told me what sins I had committed.[7]

Journalist John McCaffery went to confession to Padre Pio, also wanting prayers for some of his friends. McCaffery recalls:

So, during a pause, I began to say, "And then, Padre . . .," but he interrupted me smilingly and said: "Yes, I shall remember your friends too!"[8]

Frederick Abresch was converted after going to Padre Pio for confession. Here he describes his incredible conversion:

In November of 1928, when I went to Padre Pio for the first time, it had been a few years since I had passed from Protestantism to Catholicism, which I did out of social convenience. I did not have the faith; at least now I understand that I was merely under the illusion of having it. Having been raised in a highly anti-Catholic family and imbued with prejudices against dogmas to such a degree that a hasty instruction was unable to wipe out, I was always avid for secret and mysterious things.

I found a friend who introduced me into the mysteries of spiritism. Quite quickly, however, I got tired of these inconclusive messages from beyond the grave; I went fervently into the field of the occult, magic of all sorts, etc. . . . With self-assurance and self-importance, I used words like Reincarnation, Logos, Brahma, Maja, anxiously awaiting some great and new reality that was supposed to happen. . . . To please my wife, from time to time I still continued to approach the holy Sacraments. This was my state of soul when, for the first time, I heard of that Capuchin Father who had been described to me as a living Crucifix, working continual miracles. . . .

I decided to go and see with my own eyes. I knelt down at the confessional [and told Padre Pio that] . . . I considered confession to be a good social and educational institution, but that I did not believe in the divinity of the Sacrament at all. . . . The Padre, however, said with expressions of great sorrow, "Heresy! Then all your Communions were sacrilegious . . . you must make a general confession. Examine your conscience and remember when you last made a good confession. Jesus has been more merciful with you than with Judas."

Then, looking over my head with a stern eye, he said in a strong voice, "Praised be Jesus and Mary!" and went over to the church to hear the women's confessions, while I stayed in the sacristy, deeply moved and impressed. My head was spinning, and I could not concentrate. I still heard in my ears: "Remember when you last made a good confession!" With difficulty I managed to reach the following decision: I would tell Padre Pio that I had been a Protestant, and that although after the abjuration I was rebaptized (conditionally), and all the sins of my past life were wiped out by virtue of holy Baptism, nevertheless, for my tranquility I wanted to begin the confession from my childhood.

When the Padre returned to the confessional, he repeated the question to me: "So when was the last time you made a good confession?" I answered, "Father, as I was . . ." At that point the Padre interrupted me, saying, ". . . you last made a good confession when you were coming back from your honeymoon, let's leave everything else aside and begin from there!" I remained speechless, shaken with a stupor, and I understood that I had touched the supernatural. The Padre, however, did not leave me time to reflect. Concealing his knowledge of my entire past, and in the form of questions, he listed all my faults with precision and clarity. . . . After the Padre had brought all my mortal sins to light, with impressive words he made me understand all the gravity of these faults, adding in an unforgettable tone of voice, "You have sung a hymn to Satan, while Jesus in His ardent love has broken His neck for you." Then he gave me my penance and absolved me. . . . I believe not only in the dogmas of the Catholic Church, but also in the least of its ceremonies . . . to take away this faith, one would have to take away my life as well.[9]

Don (Fr.) Nello Castello, a priest from Padua, recalls his confessions with Padre Pio:

I went to confession to Padre Pio at least a hundred times. I recall the first time, his words both jolted and enlightened me. The counsels he gave me reflected exact knowledge of my whole life both past and future. At times he would surprise me with suggestions unconnected with the sins confessed. But later events made it clear that his counsel had been prophetic.

In one confession in 1957, he spoke five times with insistence on the same question, using different words, and reminding me of an ugly fault of impatience. Furthermore, he enlightened me on the underlying causes that provoked the impatience. He described to me the behavior I should follow to avoid impatience in the future. This happened without my having said a word about the problem. Thus, he knew my problems better than I did and advised me how to correct them.[10]

Many who came to see Padre Pio were unbelievers motivated by curiosity or the desire to mock both Padre Pio and God. Two Freemasons, who were bitterly opposed to God and the Catholic Church, made up confessions to trick Padre Pio. They wanted to desecrate the Sacrament of Penance. The two men went to confession at different times to throw Padre Pio off their trail. As each man entered the confessional and began to speak, Padre Pio stopped them and said he knew what they were doing and told each one their real sins. He told them how they committed their sins, including places and times. The men were so shocked that they repented of their sins and converted two days later.

Padre Pio believed that going to confession frequently was necessary for growth in the spiritual life. He himself went to confession at least once a week. He told his spiritual children to never go without the Sacrament of Confession for more than ten days. Katharina Tangari explains to us how Padre Pio heard confession:

> Padre Pio began with his asking us how long it had been since our last confession. This first question established contact between Padre Pio and the penitent; it suddenly seemed as if Padre Pio knew everything about us. If his [the penitent's] answers were unclear or inexact, he would correct them; we would get the feeling that . . . his eye could see our soul as it really was before God.[11]

Devil in the Confessional?

There were times when the spiritual eyes of Padre Pio discerned more than sin—at times he recognized the oppression of the enemy and did what he could to free those held in spiritual bondage. Msgr. George Pogany, a native of Hungary, lived in San Giovanni Rotondo and was an assistant to Padre Pio, handling his correspondence from 1940 to 1957. In 1989 Msgr. Pogany recalled an incident about a woman who went to Padre Pio for confession:

This is what I heard from Padre Pio's own mouth. He was hearing confession in the sacristy shortly after he received the Stigmata. There was at that time a swinging door [separating the sacristy from the main entrance of the church]. It was noon, and the people went home to dinner, and the friars closed the church. Still, there remained one woman. Padre Pio heard the confession of the woman in the sacristy. He told me, "I gave her advice, and I was about to give the absolution, but when I went to say the first words, *Ego Te,* the woman sprang up, gave a cavernous cry, and disappeared. I was frightened. I went to the door. It was swinging."

Padre Pio continued, "Padre Ignazio [the superior] was there, and I asked, 'Did you see someone go out from the church?' Padre Ignazio answered, 'No, nobody.' 'I don't know what that woman was,' said Padre Pio. 'Maybe it was the devil trying to play a trick on me.'"[12]

After Padre Pio's death, Fr. John Schug interviewed some of the older friars. They recalled a woman who seemed more than just mentally ill. She had an uncanny look in her eyes, and her face was hideous and distorted. People would run from her in fear. The woman came into the church one day and screamed out, "I am the owner of the church. I'm the only person who gives orders here." Seeing a picture of St. Michael the Archangel, who cast Satan out of heaven, she said, "You didn't win, I won!"

At that time Padre Pio was hearing men's confessions in the sacristy. When he heard the commotion, he came into the church to see what was happening. The sacristan tried to stop him, saying, "Don't go! There is a possessed woman in there."

Padre Pio told him, "Don't be afraid. Since when are we afraid of the devil?" He walked over to the woman, who was next to the women's confessional, crouching like a tigress. Padre Pio ordered her, "Get away from there!"

Suddenly the woman seemed transformed, a tigress who had turned into a kitten. She pleaded with Padre Pio, "Please don't send me away." Padre Pio responded, "All right, go away until I finish hearing confessions. Then come back." When Padre Pio came back from the sacristy, he found the woman sitting quietly. He led her to the confessional booth and heard her confession. When the woman left, her face shone like an angel's.[13]

Padre Pio often did battle with evil spirits, including exorcisms. One Sunday in May 1922, Alberto D'Apolito, who was a fourteen-year-old altar boy at the time, witnessed the following:

> After Vespers and Benediction . . . we returned to the sacristy, where we found a possessed woman, who, upon seeing Padre Pio, began to scream and curse. Padre Pio, impassive and serene, took the book in his hands, and began the exorcism amidst the screams, the curses, and the foul words of the possessed woman. Suddenly she gave forth a very loud scream, and, by an invisible force, was raised in the air to the height of three feet. At that moment, everyone began to run with fear. Padre Pio, without getting upset, continued the exorcism with faith and energy, in a ruthless struggle with the devil who, finally vanquished, freed the woman.[14]

Through the lived example and witness of Padre Pio, we see that the Sacrament of Confession is the key to heaven. We are so fortunate to have the opportunity to confess our sins. When we receive this sacrament, we not only examine our consciences but also open our minds to where we are in our lives and renew and refresh our souls.

Let's take a moment to consider the areas of our lives where we need that renewal and refreshment.

REFLECTION

How do you approach Confession? Do you take the time to examine your conscience? We don't have Padre Pio in the confessional to remind us of our sins, so it is necessary for us to properly prepare for the sacrament.

When you enter your parish church, always present yourself to the Lord in the tabernacle. Greet him with reverence and thank him for all that you receive from him each day. Even if you will not be going to Confession, take time to examine your conscience before or during Mass so that you can receive all the graces God wants to give you through Holy Communion. Each of us should have a clear, clean mind and soul as we approach the altar for Communion.

Do you ever find yourself becoming angry or mistrustful of those close to you because of the little disturbances in daily life? Have you misjudged someone or ignored the feelings of others? Are you quick to judge and slow to listen? Have you been a good friend and neighbor? Do you show your love by taking time to approach your neighbors and ask about their well-being? These are some of the questions we might ask ourselves as we examine our consciences.

When there are disputes in your family, do you take the time to listen to both sides of the story? Do you consider the feelings of others as well as your own? Do you listen to others as you expect them to listen to you?

Jesus said, "This is my commandment: love one another as I love you" (Jn 15:12). Do you live by these words? You know this is the Lord's desire. Do you do everything in your power to have peace in your life and in your family?

How deep is your well?

If today you are missing a family member, a friend, or a neighbor, give them a call and let them know how important they are to you and that you want them in your life. Don't let a moment of anger turn into a lifetime of regret. When it comes to your family, try to be a peacemaker. Don't turn a deaf ear to those who need a friend. Follow the way of the Lord. Love your family, your friends, your neighbors!

How deep is your well?

$\mathcal{P}$RAYER

May the Living Water who resides in my soul bring me refreshment and enrich my spiritual life.

Offer one Our Father, one Hail Mary, and one Glory Be.

7.

$\mathcal{P}$ERSECUTION AND CONFINEMENT

The Lord has left my soul to waste away and suffering.
My state is painful, terrible, extremely frightening. All
is darkness around and within me, darkness of the
mind, illusion of the will and distress in the memory.
All that sustains me is the thought of my faith. I am
touched by suffering in the depths of my being and at
the same time afflicted and distressed by the divine
love for which I eagerly long.

—Padre Pio

Pope Benedict XV (1854–1922), under whose reign Padre
Pio received the stigmata, looked upon the friar with a
certain benevolence. He once told a monsignor, "Padre
Pio is one of those whom God from time to time sends to
convert mankind. [We should] take on the task of making
him better known. He is not appreciated [as much] as
he deserves."[1] When he died in 1922, Pope Benedict XV
could not have imagined the suffering that was in store
for the Capuchin father he so admired.

Whereas Benedict XV had viewed Padre Pio with
kindly approval, his successor, Cardinal Ambrogio

Damiano Achille Ratti (Pope Pius XI), had a very different view. His skepticism brought Padre Pio and the Capuchins under the thumb of the local ecclesial authority, Archbishop Pasquale Gagliardi. At Christmastime in 1925, Padre Pio began to feel the effects of the false accusations being made against him. He suffered greatly, feeling alone and abandoned. Two days before Christmas, he wrote to his provincial, Padre Bernardo Apicella:

> My spirit has felt alone—totally alone—accompanied by a complete inner conviction, contrary to my will, of being abandoned by everybody. I try in vain to make acts of conformity to God. I call to him in vain. Without exception, heaven itself for me has become like bronze. I feel like I'm halfway in hell. I say halfway because in the mist of this torturous agony, I still don't feel completely without hope. . . . I feel keenly the need for a true, sincere, and intimate conversation with God, and I don't know where, and how to begin.
>
> Here is what I constantly ask of Jesus: my conversion. If I am in his disfavor, make me understand clearly, and not just suppose and guess because in this way, I will never understand a thing and much less resolve to do anything.[2]

THE CONFINEMENT

By this time, thousands of people had witnessed the bloodstained hands and the tears of Padre Pio as he served on the altar at Mass. His suffering as he endured the Passion of Christ and his fight against the attacks of the devil were evident to all, especially as he exposed the wounds on his hands, as was required of him. His pain was severe during the consecration, and his tears were uncontrollable.

Sadly, Padre Pio had detractors who spoke ill of him, even denounced him to higher ecclesial authorities. At one point, he was forbidden by the Supreme Sacred Congregation of the Holy Office, also known as the Congregation for the Doctrine of the Faith, to show his wounds. This effectively meant he could not preside over Mass in public.

Padre Pio was confined to his quarters in the monastery for two years, from June 11, 1931, to July 15, 1933. He was not allowed to descend into the church. With the exception of Mass, which he celebrated privately in the inner chapel of the monastery, Padre Pio was suspended from every ministry. When he learned the extent of the restrictions placed on him, he said, "The will of God must be done." He was also not allowed to speak with anyone outside of the monastery or to carry on in a normal way with his brother friars.[3]

This segregation from his brother friars must have been extremely difficult for Padre Pio. Not being able to work alongside them or to perform his usual duties was like a death sentence. Being locked away in another part of the monastery, alone, he must have felt that there was no one in the world who cared about him.

Have you ever been unjustly punished or made to feel alone because of a misunderstanding or because someone judged you for how you expressed your faith? How can you be more like Padre Pio and use those experiences to grow in grace?

The Cost of Obedience

When Padre Pio spoke with his brother friars, he didn't complain about the confinement and his loneliness. The archbishop and the Holy See had sworn him to silence; he couldn't tell his brothers anything. Other than asking them to take care of his spiritual children in San Giovanni Rotondo, he was silent. Always obedient!

These endless months of isolation must have affected him greatly. And yet, I sometimes wonder if Padre Pio ever came to see his isolation as a kind of blessing, for by it he gained countless hours for prayer.

We were not created to live in isolation—and by faith, we can feel the Lord always with us. The recent pandemic was a difficult, lonely time for many of us. However, even in my isolation, I recognized the blessing of having more time to pray and give thanks to the Lord for helping me, and to pray for those who were alone and struggling to survive.

But what about those who were alone and without faith? I heard many people say that when flipping through TV channels, they came across EWTN or a televised Mass. They began to watch it and returned to the faith. God definitely had a plan during COVID. Part of his plan was to toss out a net and catch some of those fish that had been swimming around endlessly, looking for deeper waters to rest in. They finally found the Living Water and came to rest in him.

We know God had a plan for Padre Pio, too. In a letter to Padre Agostino dated February 13, 1913, Padre Pio tells how "the most sweet Jesus" came to him in a spiritual locution and told him that he would suffer but that he would receive the strength to bear it: "Do not fear, I will make you suffer. I want your soul to be purified and tried by a daily martyrdom; do not be frightened if I allow the devil to torment you, the world to disgust you and your nearest and dearest to afflict you, for nothing will prevail against those who groan beneath the Cross for love of me and whom I have taken care to protect."[4]

This was a great challenge to Padre Pio's faith. The Lord was testing his fortitude and obedience above all. Padre Pio called this two-year period his "imprisonment." He offered this trial as a sacrifice to God for the salvation of souls in danger. And yet this time of confinement weighed heavily on him.

Padre Pio's Silent Intercessors

During the first year of the restrictions placed on Padre Pio, his assistant, Mary Pyle, walked fifteen miles to and from St. Michael's Shrine in Monte Sant'Angelo to pray for an end to the incarceration. A year later she again walked to the shrine, but this time she remained in the village overnight. During that time Padre Pio's case was being investigated in Rome.

During the investigation, Padre Pio's Capuchin brothers at the monastery recommended that everyone maintain a discreet silence on the matter. Their hope was to create a better climate of opinion, one that would make people in powerful positions see the goodness in Padre Pio and not assemble against him.

When you face trials, do you wait silently and patiently for the Lord to make everything right for you again? Do you turn your fear and suffering over to the Lord? Do you trust in him to make your life better again?

How deep is your well?

Pray, Hope, and Don't Worry

Mary Pyle truly loved Padre Pio and tried to live by his words, "Pray, hope, and don't worry." Mary certainly prayed and hoped, but, in fact, contrary to Padre Pio's advice, she worried every day for her beloved spiritual father. She knew how difficult this incarceration was for him.

Padre Pio did suffer greatly. His life was spent ministering to God's people in the confessional and serving on the altar, and those things had been taken away. He was concerned about the souls that would suffer in his absence. As we have seen, Padre Pio had a unique ability to touch souls. He could read hearts, and he knew the best possible way to regain a soul. During this period of confinement, he worried about what would happen to these souls if suddenly the Lord took them home without their having the advantage of his confessional. This had to weigh very heavily on Padre Pio's heart. I recall his words, "I wish there were forty-eight hours in a day to pray." Padre Pio now had all the time in the world, and I'm sure he used this time to pray for those souls who could possibly be lost.

Although he could say Mass privately, for Padre Pio the Mass was about sharing the gifts of the Lord with the people. He was concerned about the townspeople who attended his Mass every day. He knew they were suffering because of his incarceration. And in truth the whole town suffered.

THE INVESTIGATION

By July 1919 doctors were sent to examine Padre Pio's wounds. The first was Dr. Angelo Maria Merla. Dr. Merla affirmed that the priest's lesions were not the results of tuberculosis, but he could not say with any certainty what caused them without further testing. The personal physician of Pope Benedict XV, Giuseppe Bastianelli was an expert on malaria; he examined the wounds but never submitted a written report of his findings.

Detailed reports do exist from three physicians who examined Padre Pio between 1919 and 1920, including that of Amico Bignami, a professor of pathology at the University of Rome and a highly respected physician. Bignami studied Padre Pio's wounds for a period of seven days in July 1919. Luigi Romanelli, chief of staff of the City Hospital of Barletta, examined Padre Pio's wounds five times between May 1919 and July 1920.

Giorgio Festa, a surgeon in private practice, examined Padre Pio on three separate occasions. The last time was in 1925 when Padre Pio underwent a hernia operation. By this time, the Holy Office had forbidden Padre Pio to show his wounds to anyone, even a physician, without its permission. Since Dr. Festa did not have permission to examine the wounds, Padre Pio refused anesthesia for his hernia operation to ensure his hands would remain covered. However, during the course of the surgery, Padre Pio passed out from the pain, and this gave the doctor the opportunity to examine the wounds.

The upper and lower surface of Padre Pio's hands showed lesions that were clearly visible. The wounds were in the center of the palms. All the physicians who examined Padre Pio were in agreement that the wounds were circular and approximately 3/4 of an inch in diameter. The wounds consisted of a shiny viscous red membrane. They were slightly raised. When not covered with a scab or blood, they resembled a tiny button. The wounds in Padre Pio's feet were seen and described much less often than those in his hands. Festa wrote:

> On the backs of both feet and corresponding exactly in the middle of the second metatarsal, I noticed a circular lesion, red brown in color, covered by a thick, blackish scab, which had exactly the same characteristics as those described on the hands. Maybe these were a little smaller and more superficial . . . here also the skin which surrounds the lesions presents no traces of infiltration, nor swelling, nor of phlogistic [inflammatory] reactions, here also there is a slight but continued oozing of bloody serum. On the soles of the feet, and at a point which more or less corresponds to those on the back of the feet, may be seen two lesions, one in each sole, quite clear in their edges and perfectly identical to the preceding ones.[5]

Most witnesses testified that the wound in Padre Pio's side was shaped like a cross. Padre Paolino da Casacalenda believed that the first slash had come at the time of the transverberation in August 1918 and the second, along with the lesions of the hands and the feet, in September 1918.

Dr. Romanelli claimed that when he examined Padre Pio in June 1919, the side was not cruciform, but "a clean cut parallel to the ribs," about three inches long.[6] In subsequent exams, nearly everyone, including Romanelli, observed the wound in the left side, just under the nipple, in the shape of a cross. Except for an examination by an inquisitor in 1921, there were no more formal examinations of the stigmata.

THE MAKING OF A SAINT

Padre Pio surrendered so completely to the directives of his ecclesial authorities that he chose to undergo surgery without anesthesia in order not to reveal the wounds on his hands. Few of us would be willing to suffer in this way in order to remain obedient to the Holy Office. Yet he remained in silence and accepted all that was done to him.

Dr. Bignami observed that Padre Pio ate very little food. He also noted that Padre Pio was thin and pale and that his face was "illuminated by a very clear gaze." Despite the fact that he ate little, the friar seemed full of spiritual energy. Through the Eucharist, Jesus strengthened him and gave him all he needed to withstand the medical scrutiny.

These examinations must have embarrassed and upset Padre Pio. Yet he remained silent, accepting all that was done to him in accordance with the order of the Holy Office. Sadly, Archbishop Gagliardi was unmoved by his obedience. He accused Padre Pio of causing his own wounds and applying perfume to mimic the "odor of sanctity." However, these accusations, which arose after a single visit made by the archbishop in 1920 or 1921, were patently false. Padre Pio's confessor, Padre Agostino, was present at the visit and wrote the following account of what transpired:

> The archbishop arrived at the Friary around 10:30 and was greeted by me at the door of the friary. I accompanied him to room number 9. I stopped to talk with him alone since we had known each other for many years. At 10:34 Padre Pio arrived and knelt to kiss the ring of the archbishop, who was seated. When the archbishop extended his right hand to Padre Pio, I saw him bend over and kiss Padre Pio's hand which was covered. After they had exchanged a few words Padre Pio asked permission to say Mass (at that time Padre Pio was scheduled to celebrate at 11). Then the archbishop said to me, "Let's go hear the Mass." So I accompanied the archbishop to the choir. He took his seat there . . . with his breviary in his hand to say his office and watch Padre Pio as he celebrated. . . . At the end of the Mass Padre Pio did not say the Ave Maria.

The archbishop asked me why. I answered that this was a conventional Mass.

After dinner Padre Pio went to rest and we friars went into the garden . . . to take our recreation with the archbishop. After the recreation, around three, the [archbishop] had to go home and wanted to say goodbye to Padre Pio. I went up with the archbishop and we met Padre Pio in the hall. The archbishop went up to Padre Pio to speak to him. I stood somewhat aside but heard these precise words that the archbishop addressed to Padre Pio in a low voice: "Father, pray hard for a sick little niece of mine." Then Padre nodded yes and knelt to kiss the sacred ring of the archbishop. The Padre accompanied the archbishop to the stairway along with me and others.[7]

As we can see from the above account, Archbishop Gagliardi was never in Padre Pio's room or alone with him elsewhere in the monastery. He had no basis for saying that he witnessed Padre Pio applying perfume and makeup to his body. And this was, in fact, the one and only time the archbishop was at the monastery.

So, we have to ask, why did the archbishop make this false claim? At one point it appears that he believed in Padre Pio's spiritual gifts. Why else would he kiss Padre Pio's gloved hand and ask the monk to pray for his sick niece? Some have suggested that his niece was not cured, so the archbishop blamed Padre Pio. Others speculate that it was a trick to get Padre Pio to slip up.

What we do know is that after his visit, the archbishop took every opportunity to attack Padre Pio. He sent letters to the Holy Father maligning Padre Pio's character and instructed another priest to do the same. This priest, Don Domenico Palladino from San Giovanni, was one of Padre Pio's most venomous detractors. Much later, when Palladino was in his eighties, Padre Alberto D'Apolito interviewed him, asking his motivation for sending these accusatory letters. He asked Palladino, "Were you sure of what you were asserting? Didn't you think that you were lying and doing evil?"

"No!" Palladino replied. He was convinced he was doing good; he thought Padre Pio was an imposter and did not want others led astray. And, he added, "At that time I had to obey the one who gave me orders." When pressed, Palladino said that the bishop gave him these orders. Palladino justified his own conduct by saying that he was very young and didn't really think about what he was doing. He just knew he had to obey.

Later, the Holy Office investigated the matter and approached Archbishop Gagliardi to ask about the accusations. Gagliardi swore on his pectoral cross that they were true. So, we have two priests—Padre Pio and Padre Palladino—who were obedient to their bishop. Padre Pio was obedient because he trusted in the Lord. Padre Palladino, on the other hand, was obedient out of fear. While Padre Pio trusted that the Lord would make everything right, Padre Palladino trusted his unfounded feelings that Padre Pio was an imposter. Acting on those feelings, he prolonged Padre Pio's suffering.

Padre Pio's accusers continued their attacks into the early months of 1926. At that time, Archbishop Gagliardi wrote to Padre Pio's provincial, Padre Bernardo, charging that Padre Pio's spiritual children, at the priest's insistence, made confession too often and that, ignoring the orders of the Holy Office, the Capuchin was continually speaking to women in places other than the confessional and allowing them to kiss his hand.

On May 18, 1926, Padre Bernardo shared these accusations with Padre Pio, who responded as follows:

> I feel my very soul ripped up and annihilated, to the point that I can't go on. My father, what infamy they have written, knowing that they were lying, and they wanted to lie in a slanderous way. This is the thanks I get after I have spent my entire life in my sacred ministry!
>
> The persons you mentioned were never permitted access to my confessional before the [required] eight day [interval] and much less have I conferred with them elsewhere, as . . . erroneously stated. . . . As for [their] coming to kiss my hand when I am in the

confessional, God knows, and those who are found in our church know, too, how many times I yelled at them, and if I didn't succeed, am I at fault? Should I have punched them?

Now, in the face of so many slanderous and infamous accusations presented so crushingly as to create, as you could say, a dome over hell, thinking about this is enough to make me truly lose my peace and my mind, if the Lord did not come to my aid with his vigilant grace.

And now, my Father, pardon me if I have upset you, but that wasn't my intention. After all, I can't go on anymore and you are my father and in you I wanted to confide a part of the anguish that lacerates my heart![8]

When a holy person like Padre Pio brings light to a community, the devil does everything in his power to extinguish the light with more and more darkness. Pride. Envy. Slander. All very powerful weapons—but not as powerful as trust and surrender. The archbishop was determined to make Padre Pio disappear, but God had a different plan.

How would you have responded had you been in Padre Pio's shoes? What would you do if, by doing the right thing, you were afraid to bring down the wrath of the authorities upon your head?

How deep is your well?

The Truth Emerges

Over time, important information about the archbishop came to light. In the mid-1920s, Emanuele Brunatto, a faithful assistant to Padre Pio, wrote a dossier on Gagliardi, which, among other things, denounced a number of priests and religious in his archdiocese. Brunatto asserted that Gagliardi covered up their misdeeds for financial gain. The Holy Office finally opened an investigation into the matter and discovered that the archbishop was mismanaging the finances of the archdiocese.

In October 1929, Archbishop Gagliardi resigned, and Bishop Alessandro Macchi became the new administrator of the archdiocese of Manfredonia. Unfortunately, Bishop Macchi had no respect for Padre Pio either, threatening to throw him into a car in the dead of night and send him to Rome "just like he was a sack of straw."[9]

It was during this period that Padre Pio was confined to the monastery for two years. Bishop Macchi attempted to transfer Padre Pio out of the area, but the prefect of Foggia warned against this, saying that it would cause riots. Through all this, Padre Pio continued to suffer. He was unable to speak on his own behalf. In obedience, he remained silent.

Finally, in 1933, after new facts came to light, Pope Pius XI released Padre Pio from his restrictions. His Holiness said that he was misinformed about certain matters.

He went on to say that he never had anything against Padre Pio and therefore he was lifting the restrictions. This was the first time in Church history that a decree was retracted.

On July 16, 1933, Padre Pio again celebrated Holy Mass in the Church of Santa Maria delle Grazie. Among the faithful were his devoted followers who, from the first day of Padre Pio's segregation, had prayed for this happy moment.

How did Padre Pio respond to his restored freedom, which enabled him to take up his work among his spiritual children again? Let me conclude with a statement from Fr. Donatus Wynant of Welle, a Belgian priest and minister general, who on August 7, 1938, went to San Giovanni Rotondo, accompanied by Padre Agostino, to investigate all that he had heard concerning Padre Pio. Fr. Donatus wrote:

> I can, and must affirm that in all the contacts I had with Padre Pio, I was deeply moved by his practice of virtue, his serenity, his humility . . . his attitude of forgiveness that never allowed him to say a word against those who had offended him . . . his habitual recollection . . . his true affection toward his superiors . . . his perfect obedience to all ecclesiastical authorities, his sane piety, and his modesty. Personally, I have to add that I consider Padre Pio, a great saint.[10]

REFLECTION

Padre Alessio Parente, a wonderful Capuchin priest I met in 1995, was the constant companion of Padre Pio in his later years. On a certain occasion, Padre Alessio was able to get a good look at the stigmata. He said, "I had always wished to see Padre Pio's hands, but once I saw them I prayed, 'God don't ever let me see his hands again.'"[11] Padre Alessio described them as corroded and torn, reminding him of a leper's hands. At the same time that Padre Pio suffered in this way with the stigmata, he was enduring constant controversy and accusations from high-ranking officials in the Church.

If you were under attack and false accusations were being made against you, how would you respond? Would you keep silent and let the Lord take care of the matter? Would you turn the other cheek to protect the Church? Padre Pio always remained faithful and obeyed his superiors, even when they were working against him. He was a true saint in the making.

How deep is your well?

One last reflection before we move on. In this chapter we heard Padre Pio's comment, "I wish there were forty-eight hours in a day to pray." How many hours in the day do you pray? Most of us have very busy schedules. The calendars on our desks, our computers, our phones, even our watches give us reminders of appointments, meetings, lunches, vacations, and so on.

Do you know what is missing from these calendars? Every important moment in our lives is recorded on them, yet not our prayer time. How much time have you scheduled for God today? Fifteen minutes? Ten minutes? Five minutes? Any time at all? Many of us depend on our calendars to make sure we don't miss the important things in life, but we haven't scheduled time for our Creator, who gave us life. Think about that.

Padre Pio tells us that we should pray the Rosary every day. What Padre Pio is saying is that it is important to think about the things of God and to communicate with God. We certainly know how to communicate with him when we are in need. Why wait for those moments? Why not communicate with God more often? Should we say a Rosary every day? That would be nice, but with our busy schedules, it's not always possible.

Why not start off small? Take out your calendar and schedule five, ten, or fifteen minutes for God every day. What prayers will you say? How about an Our Father, Hail Mary, and Glory Be. They're prayers that we all know. Or simply take this time to talk to God about whatever is in your heart and on your mind. Ask for his help. Before you know it, those few minutes may become your favorite time of the day!

PRAYER

May the Living Water who resides in my soul bring me refreshment and enrich my spiritual life.

Offer one Our Father, one Hail Mary, and one Glory Be.

8.

$\mathcal{P}$ROTECTION IN WARTIME

The war will last very long. You will see it pass from town to town, like a river in flood, spreading destruction, blood and death! God help us!

—Padre Pio

Padre Pio made a promise to the people of his town that "no bomb would fall on San Giovanni Rotondo."[1] In order to understand how Padre Pio kept his word to the people of San Giovanni Rotondo, we first need to understand Italy's part in World War II.

In the beginning, Padre Pio did not actively denounce the Fascist prime minister Benito Mussolini. That changed when Mussolini began to force the Italian people to join the Fascist party. Without a Fascist membership card, you couldn't buy sugar, flour, or oil. Padre Pio also greatly objected to Mussolini's alliance with the German dictator Adolf Hitler. Padre Pio's biggest fear was that Hitler's hatred of Christianity would spread to Italy. Although he prayed for the conversion of Mussolini, who he felt "has done some good," he stated openly that "Hitler and Stalin are two devils and their public conversion, after so much evil, after committing so many massacres, would be a scandal. Compared with them, Nero was a little sinner!"[2]

Many Italian people believed that Hitler would win the war and that Italy would hold a prominent position in the new world order. But Padre Pio predicted that great suffering and destruction were in store. "A people chosen by God, uniting with the enemy of God. . . . This is something that must lead to punishment!"[3] (In this case he was referring not to the Jews but to the Italian Christians who had been caught up in the war effort.)

One day, while Padre Pio was discussing the war with some fellow Capuchins, he predicted, "We will retreat to Benghazi and then into the desert, then to Tripoli and then into Sicily and then into Italy."[4] Some of his brothers said they hoped this would not happen, to which Padre Pio responded, "Desire is one thing, facts are another. I speak of facts and the facts are these." His prediction was proven correct.

In 1943, when the Allies invaded Italy, Mussolini sent Padre Pio a message to pray for the country. Padre Pio replied, "So *now* you come to me after you have destroyed Italy!" He fumed, "You can tell Mussolini that nothing can save Italy now! Nothing! You have destroyed her!"[5]

Padre Pio suffered greatly during this time. He feared for the people of his country, and he suffered along with those who were starving. Although he already had a very meager diet, he gave up bread to show his solidarity with the people.

THE BOMBING OF FOGGIA

Believing that war was imminent and that Hitler would win, Mussolini had formed an alliance with Nazi Germany in 1936. After the Allied forces (England and the United States) won the North African campaign on May 13, 1943, the invasion of Europe began. With the huge Allied army and navy in the southern Mediterranean, British and American strategists decided to invade Europe from what Winston Churchill called "the soft underbelly of Europe." On July 10, 1943, Allied forces invaded Sicily and from there the mainland of Italy, where some bases were already established—including an American air base near the city of Foggia, only twenty-five miles south of San Giovanni Rotondo.

On July 22, 1943, at 9:43 a.m., the skies above Foggia suddenly darkened. Forty Flying Fortresses and more than fifty fighter planes descended on the town. By the time the bell of the town hall tolled to give the alarm, the massacre had already begun. Padre Pio's prediction that the war would bring "destruction, blood and death" came true. In Foggia alone, more than twenty thousand people—about one-third of the population—were killed.

A few nights before the invasion, Padre Pio was speaking with Alberto Cardone and some of his friends who were visiting from Pietrelcina. They were going home the following day and had come to say goodbye to the monk. Padre Pio asked, "Why are you going home? Don't you like it here?" The men said they had to return to their homes and, furthermore, they were almost out of food. Padre Pio insisted they stay, saying, "You're not going to die for one day's lack of eating."

The next morning the men went to Mass and afterward looked for Padre Pio. They were told that he was in the garden praying. When they entered the garden, Padre Pio called to them, "Children, come, let's pray."

Cardone recalled what Padre Pio said next:

> "Poor Foggia today." We didn't know what he meant. A few minutes later. . . . Planes were coming from all over the place and were going down to Foggia where they started to throw their bombs. . . . Padre Pio hadn't been in the Friary since Mass, so how did he know they were going to bomb Foggia? Padre Pio told me and my friend Bernardo, "Look for the others now and tell them I want to talk to them, because tomorrow you've got to go home. Those American planes were trying to destroy the station which is, I'm sure, destroyed, but the train will travel. It won't be at the station. When you get to Foggia, you've got to ask somebody how to get to the train."
>
> He didn't have a radio and had no way of knowing the station was destroyed. While we were praying,

we saw the planes throwing down bombs on Foggia. They unloaded the bombs and then they came up and away from Foggia making a turn as if they were going to come over us. Padre Pio told us, "Don't be afraid, they're not going to touch us, but poor Foggia." He was crying.

These planes made the run three times over Foggia, throwing a lot of bombs. Then they went away. Then Bernardo and I went to look for the other guys. Padre Pio warned us not to try to see him the next morning because the bus left at seven and if we went to Mass, we might miss the bus.[6]

When Cardone reached Foggia, he saw mangled corpses and shattered buildings. Survivors were screaming and crying. All that remained of the train station was charred and twisted debris. The train that they were to take the day before was totally destroyed. If Padre Pio had not stopped the men, they would have been on that train and would have burned to death.

Cardone and his friends now had to find another train to Benevento, from which they would make their way back to Pietrelcina. While they were debating what to do, a man in a black suit approached and asked if they needed help. They said, "We need to get to the train to Benevento, and we don't know where to go because the station is destroyed." The man replied, "The train is about to leave. You better hurry up and follow me. We've got to run, not walk." Cardone continued:

> After a while we saw the train. The train had already started to move. When the conductor saw us, he shouted, "Run! Run!" We ran over with the man in the black suit in front of us. We made it just as the last door of the train came by. We jumped on the train. The train was now in a field. We wanted to say goodbye but there was nothing but field and the man was gone. The man had not boarded the train. He stepped aside to let us on, then he wasn't there anymore. That's when we all started to cry.[7]

"No Bomb Will Fall" on San Giovanni Rotondo

So how was it that the Allied forces spared the region of San Giovanni Rotondo? Padre Pio had said that no bomb would fall on the town, but how did he prevent it?

Mary Pyle, Padre Pio's assistant, relates some stories told by airmen who visited San Giovanni Rotondo: "In July 1943, the city of Foggia and the surrounding area were at the center of an area designated for bombing. It was the twenty-sixth of the month, the feast of St. Anne. In the sky over San Giovanni Rotondo there appeared a squadron of bombers. Later, it was learned that the town's large school building had, falsely and treacherously, been reported to be a storage depot for [German] munitions. The bombing raid was unsuccessful."[8]

Why was it unsuccessful? Some airmen told Mary that they had seen a peculiar white cloud in the sky and that in the cloud were three persons—a monk with a beard, a woman holding a child in her arms, and a young man carrying a sword that dripped with blood. The bombers made two passes over San Giovanni Rotondo but were unable to release their bombs, apparently because of a jammed release switch.

After the Allied invasion, numerous American soldiers from the bases of Cerignola and Amendola came to see Padre Pio and Mary Pyle before leaving. Among the soldiers were the airmen who had taken part in the attempted bombing of San Giovanni Rotondo. Mary accompanied them to the monastery and presented them as a group to Padre Pio. When they saw him, some of them said: "Look, it's the monk we saw in the clouds on that raid. His hand was covered with fingerless gloves." And, according to Mary, when she took them into the church and they were standing before the statue of the Madonna of Graces, they said, "This is the woman that we saw holding the child in her arms."

Shortly thereafter, Mary took the soldiers to the grotto of St. Michael at Monte Sant'Angelo, a few miles outside San Giovanni Rotondo. When they saw the beautiful statue of St. Michael the Archangel, they exclaimed, "This is the young man we saw in the cloud, his sword dripping with blood!"

Imagine if you had been one of the airmen who had seen this vision in the sky. In wartime, soldiers are often given difficult orders to follow, orders that must be obeyed. How did these men experience God's mercy in the jammed switches and the vision? Have you ever experienced God's mercy at a time when you had something difficult to do?

Miracle at San Giovanni Rotondo

Let's take a moment to hear the testimony of the commander of one of these raids on San Giovanni Rotondo. During the Second World War, Bari, Italy—about 110 miles south of San Giovanni Rotondo—housed the headquarters of the US Army Air Forces' general command. The general commander of this base participated in a raid and was a witness to one of Padre Pio's miracles.

The American commanding officer was to lead a squadron of bombardiers to destroy what they believed was a depot of German war matériel located in San Giovanni Rotondo. The general commander explains what happened: "When the airplanes were near the target, me and my men saw in the sky a monk with uplifted hands. The bombs dropped away by themselves and fell into the woods. The airplanes reversed course without being maneuvered by the pilots or by the other officers."[9]

Who was the monk—and how did the miracle happen? Someone told the general, "At San Giovanni Rotondo there is a monk who works miracles," and he decided that, as soon as the country had been freed, he would go and find out if this was the same monk he had seen in the sky.

After the Allied invasion, the general went to the Capuchin monastery with some pilots. Entering the sacristy, the general saw a number of monks, one of whom he immediately recognized as the one who had stopped his airplanes. Padre Pio walked toward him and, as he approached the general, asked, "Are you the one who wanted to kill all of us?"

Reassured by the monk's lighthearted remark and kind expression, the general knelt in front of him. As usual, Padre Pio spoke to him in Italian, but the general heard him in English. The two became friends, and the general, who was Protestant, became Catholic.

REFLECTION

Can you imagine witnessing the event the commander described? Can you imagine piloting a plane when it suddenly releases its bombs and turns itself around? The general reacted by deciding, *When the war is over, I will investigate this.*

Maybe the general was one of those people who was always looking for something. His faith was not fulfilling him. Clearly the Lord led him to this place for a reason.

We see this event as an amazing miracle, and it certainly is, but I think it goes so much further. The Lord desired this general's salvation, and he used this event not only to save the people of San Giovanni Rotondo but also to gain the soul of the general. This man apparently had great faith and needed to find the path to Catholicism. When the path was put in the sky in front of him, he immediately recognized it.

Would you recognize it if the Lord sent you this message?

How deep is your well?

PRAYER

May the Living Water who resides in my soul bring me refreshment and enrich my spiritual life.

Offer one Our Father, one Hail Mary, and one Glory Be.

9.

$\mathcal{M}$ARIA L'AMERICANA

My daughter, do not travel anymore. Remain here.
—Padre Pio

Every Sunday after the Allied invasion, San Giovanni Rotondo came alive with American soldiers from the nearby air bases in Cerignola and Amendola. The American soldiers seemed to take over the village. These young, lively soldiers—as many as fifty in a group—were as brash as they could be, yet the moment they were in Padre Pio's presence, they became subdued. He extended a hand to them, and in that moment everything changed.

Many of these young soldiers went to Padre Pio for confession. Most of them only spoke English, yet conversations and confessions were complete. We know Padre Pio spoke no English, yet when these soldiers were asked, "How did you confess? Padre Pio does not speak English," they simply answered, "That's his affair. He told us what we needed to know!"

Perhaps Padre Pio's own words can explain how this was possible. "If the mission of your guardian angel is important, the mission of mine is certainly more so, because he also has to be my guide in translating languages."[1]

After visiting Padre Pio, these soldiers were invited to Mary Pyle's house for a meal before returning to their base. Mary Pyle was an American woman who lived in San Giovanni Rotondo and assisted Padre Pio. To learn more about her, we need to go back to New York in the early 1900s.

PADRE PIO'S SPIRITUAL DAUGHTER

Mary was born in New York City on April 17, 1888, to James Tolman Pyle and (Frances) Adelaide McAlpin Pyle. She was christened Adelia on September 15 of that year at the Church of the Covenant, a local Presbyterian church.

James Pyle was the owner of the Pyle Soap Company, which was the main supplier of soap in the area at the turn of the twentieth century. David McAlpin, Mary's maternal grandfather, was a prominent industrialist who had achieved great financial success through the production and sale of tobacco. He owned several large tracts of real estate in Manhattan, including one on 34th Street and Broadway, which was developed into the McAlpin Hotel. When it was built in 1912, the McAlpin Hotel was the largest hotel in the world.[2]

Mary's family lived comfortably in the world of high society. In fact, Mary sometimes wondered if it wasn't all a bit too comfortable. At any given time, the family had eight servants. Mary's circle of friends included the Rockefellers, President Calvin Coolidge, and Alexander Graham Bell.

At a young age Mary was exposed to the Catholic faith by a nanny who lived with the family. This experience led her to the Catholic Church. Mary was determined to become Catholic and sought to convince her family, especially her parents, of her intention. The discussion went back and forth for many years, and at one point her family gave in, saying she was old enough to decide. However, when Mary eventually joined the Catholic Church in 1913, her mother disowned her.

How did this society girl become the assistant to Padre Pio?

Mr. and Mrs. Pyle maintained an active interest in finding a proper spouse for Mary. Shortly before World War I, Mary fell in love, but her mother was not pleased with her suitor and proposed that Mary go to Italy to study. After all, she argued, Mary had already demonstrated an aptitude for languages and Italy seemed an ideal place to further her education. Mary's mother believed in the importance of learning other languages and would invite instructors to live with the family for four to six months at a time, until they all spoke the language fluently. Mary spoke five languages.

Mary was sent to Rome to study under the famous educator Dr. Maria Montessori. (Mary's family became Dr. Montessori's biggest benefactor and was instrumental in establishing the Montessori system in the United States.) A year later Dr. Montessori traveled to the United States and, while there, invited Mary to join her as her translator on her planned lecture tour around Europe. Mary's mother objected to this arrangement, but it was too late. Mary had already accepted the position and was on her way to Italy. While living in Barcelona with Dr. Montessori, Mary began her instructions in the Catholic faith. In 1916, at the age of twenty-eight, she became Catholic. She was baptized *sub conditione* by a Capuchin friar and received the name Mary.

MARY MEETS PADRE PIO

In her memoirs, Mary wrote that it was about 1921, while she was in London, that she first heard of Padre Pio and his stigmata. She soon came to believe in the authenticity of the friar but did not wish to visit him, reasoning that to do so would be merely to satisfy curiosity. She maintained that belief was enough.

In the summer of 1923, Dr. Montessori and Mary went to the isle of Capri, where they established residence. While they were in Capri, Mary's dear friend Rina Caterinici d'Ergin, a Romanian of the Orthodox faith, came to visit. Mary and Rina had been pupils of Dr. Montessori in

Rome. Rina told Mary she would like to meet the stigmatist Padre Pio. She wanted to ask him if it was God's will that she become Catholic. "But of course," Mary replied. "He is a Catholic, so he will say 'yes.'" But Rina dismissed this reasoning. "I want to hear it from his lips," she said. "I won't see him unless you come with me." Finally, Mary agreed to accompany Rina to meet Padre Pio.[3]

On the morning of October 3, 1923, Mary and Rina arrived in San Giovanni Rotondo. Mary met Padre Pio the next day. In later years, Mary was asked about this first encounter. Mary said that their "eyes met, and I knelt at his feet and said, 'Padre.' He put his stigmatized hands on my head and said, 'My daughter, do not travel anymore. Remain here.'"[4]

In response, Mary told Padre Pio that she had a job. However, after meeting him, she became very restless. She kept thinking about Padre Pio. One day during her travels with Dr. Montessori, Mary said to her friend and employer, "There is a saint living in this world, and I regret not being able to be near him. I wish to return to see him and would like you to accompany me."[5] Dr. Montessori readily consented to go with Mary.

When Padre Pio met with Mary and Dr. Montessori, he again said, "Remain here!" Mary took this to mean that she was to leave her current employment and settle in San Giovanni Rotondo. She agreed and built a house near the monastery in San Giovanni Rotondo. This house was known as "Mary's house."

In December 1941, when the United States entered World War II, Mary, who was an American citizen, was arrested. Fearful that she would be sent to a concentration camp, the Capuchins petitioned the minister of internal affairs in Rome, asking that Mary be sent to Pietrelcina to care for Padre Pio's father. The minister of internal affairs, a devout Catholic, permitted her to go and live in the house of Padre Pio's father.

At first Mary was not permitted to leave Mr. Forgione's home, but after a while, when the authorities saw that she was not a threat, she was free to go about the town and attend daily Mass. Mary was fluent in German and on more than one occasion was able to help herself and others when conflicts arose with the German soldiers.

SUNDAYS IN SAN GIOVANNI ROTONDO

When soldiers from nearby bases heard the stories of other soldiers who had met Padre Pio, they too had a desire to meet him. They were all instructed to go to Mary's house so that she could arrange a meeting with Padre Pio. Mary's house was open to every soldier, whether American, British, or German. When the American soldiers returned home, they brought back to the United States the first stories about Padre Pio.

Among these soldiers were some American service-women. One woman, a Native American, had the special assignment of assisting paratroopers. Mary helped set up a meeting between her and Padre Pio. To Padre Pio, the face of the young woman seemed to express an untranslatable kindness. Padre Pio said to her, "Your eyes tell the goodness of your soul." Her mother was a cradle Catholic, but her father had converted to Catholicism only four years before his death. When the young woman told Padre Pio of her father's death, he replied, "Your father has stolen paradise!" Thereafter, the young woman often came to visit Padre Pio and Mary Pyle.

After attending Padre Pio's Mass, these soldiers were very curious about the stigmata. They witnessed the wounds bleed during Mass. So the first question they had for Mary was why Padre Pio's hands bled. Mary began by explaining what the stigmata were: "The stigmata resemble the five wounds of Christ. From time to time, the scabs fall off and reveal the wounds in detail. Their contours are so precise that even under a magnifying glass one could see no edema or reddening. When soft, the scabs become detached from the edges and then from the center, until they fall off in their entirety, making way for the formation of a new scab tissue."[6]

Mary developed a strong friendship with many of these American soldiers, who grew in their faith because of Padre Pio. Prior to World War II, the only Americans who knew Padre Pio were Italian immigrants and their families. These young soldiers brought the stories of Padre Pio home with them. As a result, Padre Pio's popularity rose in America. By 1950, many Americans knew about the monk who lived on a mountain in Italy and performed miracles.

REFLECTION

Can you imagine what it would be like to meet Padre Pio and listen to the stories told by Mary Pyle and other faithful devotees?

If someone told you there was a monk who performed great miracles, would you simply accept it as truth, as Mary Pyle did? Would you question how some of these things were possible? Would you be curious to hear more?

How deep is your well?

Let's stop for a moment and think about the deep faith of Mary Pyle. Mary was in many ways like Padre Pio, born with a great love for Jesus in her soul. Hand-in-hand with her nanny she went to the Catholic church, and there she opened her eyes and her heart to the Lord. She knew from the moment she was in the presence of the Blessed Sacrament that she was in the house of the Lord. No one told her; she just knew it. She felt his presence.

From her early years, Mary formed a relationship with the Lord and wanted to become a part of his life. She gave up everything to be with him. Many people think Mary became Catholic when she met Padre Pio. No, she was already Catholic, but meeting Padre Pio stirred something in her soul that caused an unexplained restlessness. When Padre Pio asked Mary a second time to remain in San Giovanni Rotondo, that restlessness gave way to a calm that brought her to the real purpose of her life.

If you lived in luxury, if you had eight servants at your beck and call, if you dined at the summer homes of American presidents, would you make the decisions Mary made? Would you give that life up to serve the Lord on a mountain in Italy beside a holy monk?

How deep is your well?

$\mathcal{P}$RAYER

May the Living Water who resides in my soul bring me refreshment and enrich my spiritual life.

Offer one Our Father, one Hail Mary, and one Glory Be.

10.

$\mathcal{P}$ADRE PIO'S DREAM

This evening my earthly work has begun. I bless you and all those who will contribute to this work which will become bigger and more beautiful.

—Padre Pio

Padre Pio had a dream. Not one dream, but two dreams—or you might call them parallel dreams. He wanted to build a hospital called La Casa Sollievo della Sofferenza (Home for Relief of Suffering), and alongside it he wanted to establish prayer groups that would intercede for the sick and the hospital staff. These prayer groups would form a global, lay-run spiritual movement, supporting the work of the hospital.

Although Padre Pio had this dream long before World War II, it would not become a reality until after the war. In fact, many of the American soldiers who met Padre Pio during the war went home and told their families about the planned hospital, and donations began arriving shortly after. So many donations arrived that Padre Pio put Mary Pyle in charge of them.

The dream for this great medical center had very humble beginnings. Let's go back to 1920, to the creation of the first hospital in San Giovanni Rotondo, the Hospital of St. Francis.

THE HOSPITAL OF ST. FRANCIS

In 1920, a teachers' strike in Italy led to riots between the Socialist left and the Fascist right. In the autumn of 1920, San Giovanni Rotondo got caught up in the violence. The Socialists were trying to form a Soviet regime. They blamed the poverty in Italy on the Church and its clergy. In Foggia and nearby San Giovanni Rotondo, Socialist legislators threatened to turn all the churches into barns. The peasants backed the Socialists, while the landowners supported the Fascists.

On August 15, the Feast of the Assumption, Padre Pio went to the main square of San Giovanni Rotondo to bless the veterans in procession. In the following weeks tensions increased, and after the Socialists gained more seats than the Fascists, the Fascists disputed the election. Violence erupted, and soldiers were brought in to preserve order.

In October, Francesco Morcaldi, mayor of San Giovanni Rotondo, called on Padre Pio for help. He knew the people would listen to the monk. Padre Pio told the mayor, "You've got to pacify the people." Padre Pio suggested that he speak to the leaders on both sides and try to calm them down.

A few days later, Padre Pio put a program together to protect the citizens of San Giovanni Rotondo and to give them a bigger voice in the city government. He called for a municipal office of labor that would improve the plight of rural workers, the establishment of agricultural schools in mobile units, and increased aid to children of soldiers who had died in the war. New roads, sidewalks, telephone networks, and public toilets would be built. Finally, a city hospital would be constructed, offering free medical care to the poor.

As soon as this proposal was approved, Padre Pio began setting up the hospital. With the consent of his superiors, he actively began to solicit funds. Then an amazing thing happened. An anonymous donor gave Padre Pio fifteen thousand lire to purchase the property on which the hospital would be built. The doors of the Hospital of St. Francis opened in 1925.

Padre Pio's genius saved the people and helped build up the town of San Giovanni Rotondo. He did what the politicians could not do: he brought peace to the people of the area. Padre Pio was always there for the people, not only as a priest, but as a man who believed in the people and chose to serve them in any way he could. Perhaps that is why so many young soldiers went home to their families and presented Padre Pio's dream. They all believed that La Casa Sollievo della Sofferenza was a dream that needed to be fulfilled.

PADRE PIO'S PRAYER GROUPS

Padre Pio first started organizing informal prayer groups in nearby Foggia. In 1947, he announced, "It is time to unite both intentions and actions, to offer our Lord collective prayers imploring his mercy for humanity that appears to have forgotten him."[1] Padre Pio then established formal groups that met monthly in twenty-three Italian cities. The local bishops gave their consent, and each group was instructed to pray for the pope, Padre Pio's ministries, world peace, and the intentions of the group members. Padre Pio directed that a priest be assigned to each group as a spiritual advisor.

In the meantime, the rest of his dream was about to come true.

Has God ever given you a dream, a deep desire to do something big for him? Sometimes those dreams take a lot of faith, trust, and perseverance . . . and sometimes they take time. But don't be afraid to do big things for God—his dreams for us are almost always bigger than the dreams we have for ourselves, and if the dream is from him, he will give us what we need to accomplish it!

La Casa Sollievo della Sofferenza

In the spring of 1947, Padre Pio blessed the first stone to be used in construction of the new hospital. On May 19, ground was broken, and construction began. About a year later, in the summer of 1948, economist Barbara Ward wrote a report on the postwar reconstruction in Italy in her magazine, *The Economist*. Her fiancé, Sir Robert Gillman Allen Jackson, was deputy director of field operations of the United Nations Relief and Rehabilitation Administration (UNRRA).

While traveling through southern Italy, Ward heard about Padre Pio from her friend the Marquess Patrizi. A devout Catholic, Ward wanted to learn more about Padre Pio and his ambitious project. On her way to Taranto, she decided to stop in San Giovanni Rotondo with the Marquess and Marchioness Patrizi to meet Padre Pio.

When they arrived in San Giovanni Rotondo, they attended Padre Pio's Mass and were deeply moved. Next they met with Dr. Guglielmo Sanguinetti, one of the first shareholders in the hospital. He told them how land had been donated for the Casa and that one thousand shareholders had put up one thousand lire each for a total of one million lire to start the project. Each shareholder signed a document renouncing any future profits from the hospital.

Ward was very impressed with how construction of the hospital had gotten under way. It was obvious that the project would need more money and more donors. Ward had an idea, which she presented to her fiancé, Robert Jackson. Since the UNRRA was providing funds to rehabilitate the region of Foggia, was it possible that La Casa Sollievo della Sofferenza would qualify for help? Prior to the war, many of the hospitals and medical services in the south of Italy were in deplorable condition. With the onset of war, conditions only worsened. Foggia and most of the area around it was completely destroyed by bombing, and soon after, the area was swept by an epidemic of typhoid and malaria.

Padre Pio was furious when the Italian government granted only 250 million lire, a fraction of the original request, to begin construction of the hospital. Thanks to the UNRRA, the funds to start the project became available. But that was only a portion of what was needed. Those young soldiers who went home to the United States and other countries were the ones who spread the word among their families and friends, and they were the ones who really built the hospital.

On July 26, 1954, the outpatient clinic was blessed by Padre Pio and opened for business. On May 5, 1956, nine years after they had broken ground, the hospital was finally completed. At the ceremony, which was attended by Archbishop Andrea Cesarano, Padre Pio blessed the plaque naming the hospital for former New York mayor and current director of the UNRRA Fiorello LaGuardia (to fulfill the terms of the grant). However, whenever he spoke of the hospital, Padre Pio insisted on calling it La Casa Sollievo della Sofferenza, the name he had chosen years before.

When the Casa opened, it hosted a symposium on cardiac surgery. Eminent heart surgeons from all over the world came and admired the institution that Dr. Gustav Nylin of Sweden, president of the European Society of Cardiology, called "a magnificent work of charity."

Padre Pio charged the doctors, "Bring God to the sick. It will be more valuable than any treatment. . . . You have the mission of curing the sick but if at the patient's bedside you do not bring the warmth of loving care, I fear that medicine will not be of much use."[2]

REFLECTION

This story spans decades. It began with the need for better health care, and from that need emerged an even greater dream that would make San Giovanni Rotondo known worldwide for its amazing Casa Sollievo della Sofferenza.

Many prestigious doctors from around the world have volunteered their time to serve the people who come to the health center. I have visited the hospital many times as a board member of the Padre Pio Foundation of America. The work they do is very important.

Being a part of that work is a most rewarding experience. At present, generous benefactors are raising funds for five hundred much-needed beds and have donated new, advanced medical equipment to help the doctors provide the best possible care for the people who go there from around the world for special medical needs. This impressive hospital on the mountain can be seen from miles away as you approach San Giovanni Rotondo.

Fulfilling the second part of Padre Pio's dream, the prayer groups continue to pray for the work of the hospital—that every patient will be healed both physically and spiritually. I have met with many of these groups in my work as a pilgrimage tour operator, foundation board member, and writer. The members of these prayer groups are some of the most devoted people in the world.

Today there are more than three thousand Padre Pio prayer groups, with more than three million members. Would you like to be a part of one of these prayer groups? You can find out more at www.padrepio.org/pray/our-padre-pio-prayer-group or www.padrepio.com/ourwork/prayer-groups/.

How do I sum up this chapter? I think the most important takeaway is that Padre Pio, aside from his stigmata and miracles, had a heart for the people. God inspired him to do great things because this simple, humble man only wanted to serve the Lord and serve his people. He had a very important role to play in the lives of the people of San Giovanni Rotondo. From this tiny village Padre Pio showed the world how to love the Lord.

How can you best serve the Lord through generosity and prayer? Has Padre Pio shown you how to bring peace into your life and the lives of others? Has your faith increased as a result of hearing Padre Pio's words?

How deep is your well?

$\mathcal{P}$RAYER

May the Living Water who resides in my soul bring me refreshment and enrich my spiritual life.

Offer one Our Father, one Hail Mary, and one Glory Be.

11.

MIRACLES AND RECOLLECTIONS

Let us always humble ourselves and acknowledge that
we are nothing if we lack the Divine assistance.

—Padre Pio

When people first hear about Padre Pio, they are naturally
curious about the miracles associated with him, but those
are not the most important part of Padre Pio's life. Nothing in Padre Pio's life was more important than choosing
to suffer the Passion and Crucifixion of the Lord every day
of his life for fifty years through the stigmata.

The glossary of the *Catechism of the Catholic Church*
defines a miracle as "a sign or wonder, such as a healing
or the control of nature, which can only be attributed
to divine power." It is an event not explicable by natural
or scientific laws and so is considered to be the work of
a divine agent. For example, the miracles of Jesus were
messianic signs of the presence of God. These miracles
pointed to Jesus as the Messiah.

Padre Pio was a simple, humble man that the Lord
worked through to perform wonderful miracles. Many of
those for whom Padre Pio interceded in prayer received

miraculous answers. Of course, many for whom Padre Pio prayed did not receive a miracle. Why did some receive a miracle and others not? Only the Lord can answer that question.

Sometimes these favors were very small, even a bit trivial—yet they showed Padre Pio's care for his spiritual children. One spiritual daughter was holding a letter from him when a strong wind came along and ripped it from her hand, blowing it into a meadow. The letter came to a stop and settled on a stone just before reaching the valley. Miraculously, the woman was able to retrieve the letter. The next day, she met Padre Pio, who told her: "You have to pay attention to the wind next time. If I hadn't put my foot on the letter, it would have flown far away into the valley."

Padre Pio's spiritual children frequently sent messages to him, placing their friends and family in his care. His fatherly protection sometimes extended over many years. One especially persistent poor widow from Bologna traveled with her five children to San Giovanni Rotondo to ask Padre Pio to accept her as his spiritual daughter and to keep her children in his prayers. Her request made, she returned home and proceeded for the next five years to pray for Padre Pio's intercession for the protection and blessing of her children.

After five years, she was able to return to San Giovanni Rotondo, where Padre Pio heard her confession. When she repeated her desire for protection for her children, Padre Pio responded—kindly, if a bit gruffly—"How many times do you intend to ask me that?" She told him she did not understand. "You have asked that of me every day for the last five years!" he replied.

Humility was important to Padre Pio. He showed special concern for humble people who would rather bear their suffering than ask the Lord for a miracle. Many times, he asked a person if they wanted to be healed. Those who responded, "If it is the will of God," were the ones who were first in Padre Pio's heart. He wanted humble people to experience the wonders of the Lord.

This chapter contains several stories of Padre Pio's sons and daughters who turned to him for healing prayers. One such person was Padre Agostino.

PADRE AGOSTINO, THE "CONSOLING ANGEL"

Padre Agostino of San Marco in Lamis was Padre Pio's spiritual director. The letters of Padre Pio reveal that the two friars were very close and that Padre Agostino advised Padre Pio in many matters. He was the one who gave Padre Pio the courage to go on when he experienced the long dark nights. He was known as Padre Pio's "consoling angel." Some have suggested that Padre Pio did not have confidence in Padre Agostino. They say Padre Pio felt that his spiritual director did not understand him, but an excerpt from a letter to Padre Benedetto in October 21, 1912, shows the contrary: "The Father Lecter has always been my ordinary director, and nobody knows my interior state as well as he does. I have had frequent recourse to him and have opened up to him all the wounds of my soul, without any reticence or fear; something which has not been possible to do with others and which is not possible for me to do now. I beg you not to ask me the reason."[1]

Padre Agostino left this recollection of Padre Pio:

Padre Pio suffered and prayed for all and in a special way for the Vicar of Jesus Christ. Very often the Lord sends spiritual and bodily sufferings for salvation and the good of souls. Padre Pio once told me that he had suffered for a particular individual for almost two months. He said to me, "I don't know the reason for this, but I suffer." When I was getting ready to leave for Genoa for the hospital, I stopped to see Padre Pio and he was in bed. He told me, "My Father, go in peace, because you have someone who is praying and suffering for you." I answered, "Let's divide the suffering." He replied, "Don't give it another thought." All went well with me at the hospital and all thanks are due to Padre Pio who suffered and prayed.[2]

BR. CHRISTOPHER AND A HEALING MIRACLE

Padre Pio prayed for his spiritual children all over the world. One such spiritual child was a Capuchin brother named Christopher who lived in Australia. As a patient at Sydney Hospital, Br. Christopher witnessed a miraculous healing through the intercession of Padre Pio.

One of the other patients in the ward with Br. Christopher was a young man, about twenty years of age, who had a good job as a clerical worker at the headquarters of Peters Ice Cream Factory in Redfern, Sydney. He had been in the hospital for quite some time with a condition that caused his temperature to rise abnormally high, so much so that the nurses had to pack his body in ice to reduce his fever. He was also unable to hold down any food. His condition mystified the medical staff. Shortly after Br. Christopher's arrival in the hospital, the young man's condition began to deteriorate rapidly.

One night around midnight, the staff realized that the young man's end was near, so they summoned his family and girlfriend to the hospital. Since he was Catholic, the Catholic chaplain from St. Mary's Cathedral, Fr. Edmund Campion, was called. After Fr. Campion visited the young man, he went to Br. Christopher's bedside and said to him, "Please pray for this young man who is in your ward. He is leaving us tonight. He is not expected to last until morning."

Br. Christopher promised Fr. Campion that he would do so. After the chaplain left, Br. Christopher remembered the picture he had of Padre Pio. He had read accounts of miracles occurring after a picture of Padre Pio was placed under the pillow of a sick person. Br. Christopher gave the picture to the young man's family and told them about the holy life of Padre Pio. They thanked Br. Christopher and said they would place the picture under the sick man's pillow.

The following morning Br. Christopher woke to find the hospital staff around the bed of the young man, who appeared to be strong and healthy. The medical workers were startled by his apparent good health. He was able to sit up and eat his breakfast. After breakfast, the young man got out of bed and spoke to Br. Christopher for the first time. He said, "I want to thank you for the picture of Padre Pio. I feel sure that it saved my life." The young man was released from the hospital several days later, and Br. Christopher shortly thereafter.[3]

Ray Ewen, Padre Pio's American Friend

As we have seen, during World War II many American soldiers met Padre Pio. If you read my first book, *Welcoming the Christ Child with Padre Pio*, you will remember that my friend Ray Ewen was one of those soldiers and that, in fact, he served Mass with Padre Pio on several occasions.

Although I was already familiar with Padre Pio when I met Ray, Ray's devotion and love for the monk truly inspired me and led me on the road to a great devotion for him. And there are things about Ray and Padre Pio that I did not know until recently. For example, I knew that Ray had a rosary that was blessed by Padre Pio, but I didn't know that there was a miracle associated with the rosary. Here is Ray's story:

> I met Padre Pio during World War II, when I was stationed in Cerignola, not far from San Giovanni Rotondo. I was able to attend Padre Pio's Mass and even visit with him in the garden of the monastery, where he would sometimes have his lunch. Meeting Padre Pio was a blessing that has remained with me my entire life. When I returned home to New York after the war was over, I used every opportunity to tell others about Padre Pio. I have been a parishioner at the Sacred Heart parish in Queens for more than sixty years. A number of years ago, our pastor's sister, who was a Dominican nun, asked me if she could borrow the rosary that I have, which was blessed by Padre Pio. I agreed and she took it to where she worked at Mary Immaculate Hospital in Jamaica, New York. Later, when she returned it, she told me that one of the patients in the hospital heard about the rosary and asked her if he could pray with it. He was healed, for when he went into surgery to have a cancerous tumor removed, it had disappeared.[4]

Ray is one of those simple, humble people Padre Pio loved so much. Dear Ray, I hope you are enjoying Padre Pio's company in heaven!

MY FRIEND FANNY

Miracles can happen anywhere—even in my hometown, Staten Island, New York. Let me tell you about my friend Filomena (Fanny) Marro. Fanny and I have been friends for years. We are both parishioners of Our Lady of Pity Church. Fanny knew about Padre Pio as a young girl in her native Italy, and she thought of him often when she came to America. After his death, Fanny began to pray to him. This is Fanny's story:

> I went to my doctor for a checkup of my thyroid. The doctor told me he felt a lump and that I must go for a sonogram. The sonogram showed a lump, so he said I needed a biopsy. I was very worried, and I prayed every day to Padre Pio that the lump would not be cancerous.
>
> I went for the biopsy, and while I was on the table, the doctor began to laugh. I was upset at this and asked him why he would laugh about something so serious. He replied that there was nothing there for him to biopsy . . . he had nowhere to place the needle. The lump had disappeared. I am convinced that Padre Pio answered my prayer.[5]

And so am I!

BEHIND THE IRON CURTAIN

From behind the Iron Curtain, a thirteen-year-old boy from Czechoslovakia reached out to Padre Pio for help to become a priest. This is Fr. Paul Hancko's story:

> As a six-year-old lad, I heard Our Lord's call to be a priest. It was a great grace to receive such an invitation. Yet early in life I realized the impossibility of studying theology in Czechoslovakia, so when I was about thirteen years old, I wrote to Padre Pio, "Padre, please help me to become a priest and if I cannot study at home, please help me to get abroad." I received a handwritten note that Padre Pio was praying for me.
>
> In 1976, as an immigrant, I arrived in Canada, where I began my studies required for ordination, and on August 25, 1989, by the grace of God and through the intercession of our Blessed Mother and Padre Pio, I was ordained a priest. I am very, very happy to be a priest and to belong to the Church which has so many, many saints in every age but especially in our own time. Padre Pio, thank you![6]

PADRE FEDERICO

Padre Federico of Macchia Valfortore was one of Padre Pio's seminary students. Padre Pio also acted as his spiritual director. Padre Federico recalls:

> Padre Pio was always praying, night and day. His main teaching place for us was the choir, where he spent

long hours of the day on his knees as a faithful wor-
shiper of Jesus in the Blessed Sacrament. In our midst
he prayed and responded, always holding his rosary in
his right hand. In the refectory, after having hurriedly
and listlessly swallowed a few mouthfuls, he continued
to pray. He used to say, "I wish the day had forty-eight
hours in which to pray." In fact, he never left the choir
until midnight. When he went to bed we felt him to be
always keeping watch. His whole day was a continuous
dialogue with God.[7]

JORGE CONTRERAS: A HEALING OF THE HEART

Jorge Contreras kept Padre Pio's prayer card close to his
heart for twenty years. This is Jorge's story:

About twenty years ago I attended a seminar given
by a priest who had just returned from a trip to San
Giovanni Rotondo. His testimony about Padre Pio was
very inspiring and since that time I have developed a
very close relationship with Padre Pio. I keep a small
Padre Pio prayer card in the left pocket of my shirt
at all times. Every night I place it on my night table
before I go to bed. I obtained a master's degree in the-
ology and pastoral ministry from Barry University and
I am also a certified public accountant. My wife and I
have been active parishioners at St. Timothy Catholic
Church in Miami, where we head the evangelization
ministry. I also teach Bible classes on Tuesdays.

In 2010, I was diagnosed with severe aortic stenosis. My aortic valve should have had an opening of 3 cm and mine showed only .75. To confirm the findings, my cardiologist, Dr. Hugo Garcia, ordered a transesophageal echo test. The test showed the same results. My doctor explained to me that I was going to have to have open-heart surgery. I met the doctor who was going to perform the surgery, Dr. Niberto Moreno, at Baptist Hospital of Miami. When he saw the results of the echo test, he characterized the aortic stenosis as "critical."

Before the surgery, I had to have one other procedure, a heart catheterization. The procedure would take a close look at my arteries in order to determine the entry point for the open-heart surgery. If my arteries were in good shape, the surgeon would go through the side of my chest. If the coronary arteries were obstructed, the center of my chest would have to be opened for the surgery.

The heart catheterization procedure was performed at South Miami Hospital on April 12, 2011. As I was coming out of the sedation, my cardiologist, Dr. Garcia, said to me, "Mr. Contreras, what have you done?" I did not understand what he meant and was afraid that he had bad news for me. "I have not done anything. But I have prayed a lot," I replied. "Well, keep praying," my doctor said. "Your aorta valve now shows a 1.44 cm opening. You do not need heart surgery." I had been praying to Padre Pio since January, asking only that my coronary arteries would be healthy. Well, Padre Pio went all the way for me![8]

DANILO GANZON: PRAY, HOPE, AND DON'T WORRY

Here is the compelling story of Danilo Ganzon, who also experienced the miraculous intercession of Padre Pio:

I learned about Padre Pio through a newsletter called *Pray, Hope, and Don't Worry*, which I found in the church vestibule at Good Shepherd Parish in San Diego. I attended the Mother of Perpetual Help novena at my parish and one Tuesday night at the novena, when I looked at the picture of Our Mother of Perpetual Help, I seemed to see Padre Pio looking at me.

In February 2006, I had a hemorrhagic stroke after having a heated argument with my sister. I was lying unconscious on the floor when paramedics came and rushed me to the hospital. The right side of my brain was bleeding, and the left side of my body was paralyzed. It was uncertain whether I would live through the night.

I remained in a coma for three weeks in the intensive care unit. The neurosurgeons told my family to look for a nursing home for me because even if I came out of the coma, I would be nothing but a vegetable. I did come out of the coma, and I was able to walk and to speak with no difficulty. During my hospitalization I could always feel the presence of Padre Pio and Mother Mary with me.[9]

KENNY KEEGAN: MIRACLE OF THE MIND

One quick read and Kenny Keegan's life was changed:

I graduated from Sheffield Hallam University in York-shire in the north of England in 1983. At that time, I lived in a rented room above a bookshop, which had a lot of Marxist, anarchist, feminist, and communistic books. I looked to science and reason rather than faith to explain human existence, and I had read a lot of Marx and Freud. I considered myself an atheist and a Marxist.

The bookshop also had a variety of other kinds of secular reading material and had a contract to supply the city library with books. One night while browsing through the stacks, I came across John McCaffery's *Tales of Padre Pio.* I read the book at one sitting and was deeply impressed.

The next morning, I received a letter from my mother in Scotland containing a Padre Pio prayer card and relic. At that time, I was scared and uncertain of the future. I decided to make the prayer novena to Padre Pio, to ask for guidance in my life. Soon after, I won a scholarship to study for a postgraduate degree in Glasgow, Scotland.

Padre Pio has been my protector and benefactor ever since, and has never failed me even in my darkest times. I love and thank him from the bottom of my heart for helping me to reaffirm the beauty and peace of my Catholic faith. Viva Padre Pio![10]

Nicola La Banca: A Thrown Shoe

Nothing gets past Padre Pio.

Nicola La Banca lived in Pietrelcina. He was a childhood friend of Padre Pio. One day he had a terrible toothache. The pain was so intense he was unable to fall asleep. Nicola and his wife Philomena had a picture of Padre Pio on their wall. Philomena said to her husband, "Nico, keep calm. Invoke Padre Pio and you will see that you will soon feel better." Instead of calming him, her words annoyed Nicola and he became angry. "So now I have to invoke Padre Pio?" he exclaimed. Cursing, he picked up a shoe and threw it at the picture.

Several years later, Philomena and Nicola made a trip to Padre Pio's monastery in San Giovanni Rotondo. They both went to confession to Padre Pio. After Nicola finished his confession, Padre Pio asked him, "What else?" Nicola replied that there was nothing else to say. "Think carefully," Padre Pio said. "I have confessed everything," Nicola answered.

"Nico, when you threw the shoe in my face in Pietrelcina, did you think I wouldn't feel the blow in San Giovanni Rotondo?" Padre Pio asked. Suddenly Nicola remembered throwing his shoe, and he was deeply embarrassed. "But I had a very painful toothache," he answered. "Yes, but why did you want to take it out on me?"[11] As many of his spiritual children would testify through the years, nothing could be hidden from Padre Pio.

FAITH LIKE A MUSTARD SEED–OR ALMOND TREE

In the spring, San Giovanni Rotondo comes to life with the blossoming of beautiful almond trees. Each year, the peasants await this event because the blossoming means the harvest is near, and this is the peasants' only form of income.

One year the blossoms were so abundant they showed promise of an exceptionally good harvest. But as the time of the harvest approached, thousands of voracious caterpillars arrived and devoured the leaves and flowers. They didn't even spare the nut shells. At first the peasants worked around the clock to stop the infestation, but after two days they stopped trying. In despair, they turned to Padre Pio. He decided the best thing to do was to bless the trees. He put on his sacred vestments and stood by a window in the monastery and started to pray. When he finished praying, he took holy water and made the Sign of the Cross in the air, in the direction of the trees.

The next day, the caterpillars had disappeared, but the almond trees looked like sticks. It was a disaster; it seemed the harvest was lost. But what happened next is incredible.

The trees produced the most abundant harvest—a harvest like the peasants had never seen before. They couldn't understand how it was possible that trees without flowers could produce fruit. How could fruit come from trees that looked like sticks?

Scientists have never been able to explain this phenomenon. And yet, Padre Pio reminds us, "If you have faith the size of a mustard seed, you will say to this mountain, 'Move from here to there,' and it will move" (Mt 17:20).

Do you have that kind of faith? Can your faith move mountains?

How deep is your well?

ℛEFLECTION

While the Church sees miracles as "a sign or wonder, such as a healing or the control of nature, which can only be attributed to divine power," I see miracles as something else. I see the things the Lord does for us every day as the small miracles in life.

Think of how many times you call on the Lord during the day. We ask him to help us get through this or that. These are not extraordinary things; they are the ordinary things in our life that sometimes become overwhelming in this hectic world we live in. So, who do we turn to when we need help with these things? The Lord! And he always answers us, though it may not always be the answer we want. These are the little miracles in life.

The miracles recounted in this chapter are extraordinary, and certainly very few people will experience such miracles in their lifetime. And yet it strengthens our faith to hear about such wondrous events, and it's reassuring to know there is someone to call on when we need miraculous intervention.

Has there ever been a time in your life when your well of faith ran deep enough that you asked the Lord for a miracle—not just to avoid your own suffering or difficulty, but to help someone else?

How deep is your well?

$\mathcal{P}$RAYER

May the Living Water who resides in my soul bring me refreshment and enrich my spiritual life.

Offer one Our Father, one Hail Mary, and one Glory Be.

12.

$\mathcal{T}$HE JOURNEY HOME

I shall stand at the gates of paradise until all my spiritual children have entered.

—Padre Pio

About three months before Padre Pio's death, his stigmata emitted less and less blood until, by the time he died, on September 23, 1968, the five wounds had closed completely. They had been a part of him for fifty years.

All his life, Padre Pio's spiritual gifts had been spent in service of God's people. He had been a man of prayer and a champion in the confessional. He spent countless hours listening to confessions, his eyes looking into souls. He made each penitent aware of the wrong they had done, and when the confession was complete, they were at peace with the Lord. Even those whom Padre Pio did not absolve from their sins came back when they realized that the only road to heaven was the one Padre Pio offered them in the confessional.

His life of prayer led to phenomenal miracles. The Lord granted these miracles because Padre Pio was so humble, and he liked to ask for miracles for humble people. One such person was a young woman who was blind from birth. When Padre Pio asked her if she wanted to see, she said, "Yes, if that is the will of the Lord!" Padre Pio interceded for humble people like this who put God's will before their own.

Padre Pio always remained in close contact with the Holy Spirit, and he possessed extraordinary gifts of healing, bilocation, levitation, prophecy, miracles, abstinence from both sleep and nourishment, the ability to read hearts, the gift of tongues, and the gift of conversions. Padre Pio cried abundant tears of love; he loved the Lord deeply and wanted to live his life only for him.

And so, at the end of his life, Padre Pio's greatest desire was to go home to the Lord. Many times in his life he prayed for the Lord to take him home, not because he wanted the pain and suffering to go away—no, he gladly suffered for the Lord—but because he wanted to be constantly in the presence of the Lord, whom he loved more than anyone and anything in his life.

Padre Pio had suffered greatly for the Lord. Every day he fought demons and endured almost unbearable agony, all for the love of the Lord. He willingly accepted this call because he knew not many would choose to defend the Lord in this way. The Lord chose Padre Pio to be a champion for good in the world, and young Francesco rose to the challenge.

Many who met Padre Pio asked him to be their spiritual father, and he gladly accepted them as spiritual children. Padre Pio promised that he would not enter the gates of paradise until every one of his spiritual children was there. I'm sure he waits at heaven's door to greet each one of them.

While there are many different ways I could have started this book, I can honestly say that there is only one way to end it. Beyond the miracles, beyond the confessional, there is the man who bore the wounds of Christ and suffered the taunts of the devil every day. For fifty years Padre Pio said Mass and relived the Passion of Christ. His parish priest in Pietrelcina called Padre Pio's Mass "an incomprehensible mystery."

I often wish that I had been able to attend one of Padre Pio's Masses. I'd like to introduce you to a man who witnessed one firsthand; listen closely as he describes how Padre Pio celebrated Mass.

WILLIAM MAURICE CARRIGAN

William Maurice Carrigan was an American from Iowa. He taught psychology at the Catholic University of America in Washington, DC, until he began his work with the Red Cross at the time the United States entered World War II. He served as the field director of the American Red Cross in Italy. He traveled with the 5th Army Air

Force and was stationed with them at a base close to San Giovanni Rotondo.

Upon arrival at the base in October 1943, William heard stories about a monk who lived on a mountain and who bore the wounds of Christ. Some young soldiers who had met Padre Pio when they were searching for eggs near San Giovanni Rotondo told Carrigan about this amazing man. Many other soldiers told Carrigan that they would like to meet Padre Pio, but they had no way to get to him. After hearing their stories, Carrigan, who was a devout Catholic, said he also would like to meet the monk.

On a blistery cold, snowy morning, Carrigan gathered twenty of these soldiers, loaded them into a Red Cross truck, and headed for San Giovanni Rotondo. When they arrived, they found that Padre Pio had already started Mass.

Carrigan observed Padre Pio very closely and saw that the monk was in severe pain. It appeared to be physical suffering. He noticed that Padre Pio moved constantly, "shifting his weight from side to side," and that he leaned on the altar, as if he were trying to relieve the pain in his feet.[1]

At that time, Carrigan knew nothing about Padre Pio's stigmata. But when Padre Pio took off his gloves during Mass, the bleeding wounds on his hands were exposed. At the consecration, Padre Pio had difficulty speaking the words, "This is my body." He "would start and repeat—biting [the words] off with a clicking of his teeth as if in great pain." When the priest reached for the chalice, his hand jerked back violently "because of the pain in the wound which was fully visible to me." His face kept twitching, and tears rolled down his cheeks. After the consecration, his suffering subsided.

After Mass, Carrigan went into the sacristy to meet Padre Pio. As the monk approached, Carrigan knelt before him. Padre Pio reached down, and lifted Carrigan by the elbows, and said, "Americano?" Carrigan replied, "Si, si, Padre." Padre Pio told Carrigan that his was the first American military group that he had met since the war began. He indicated that he was delighted to meet them.

And then something amazing happened. Padre Pio allowed Carrigan to kiss his ungloved hand. Carrigan recalled that "the scales of the blood crystals were rough." He said that he experienced a pleasant aroma, which he thought might have been the scent of a medication (more likely, the fragrance of holiness). Padre Pio then gloved his hand and extended it for the other soldiers to kiss.

Carrigan and Padre Pio became very close, personal friends. On one occasion, Padre Pio invited Carrigan to stay overnight at the monastery. Carrigan slept in the cell just across from Padre Pio's cell. On other occasions, he invited Carrigan to sit with him in the choir loft and pray.

When Padre Pio knelt, he held on to Carrigan's arm and continued to hold on to his arm while he prayed, letting go only when he went back to his seat.

Whenever Carrigan spoke of his first meeting with Padre Pio, he always said he was very moved by the experience. In later years he would say, "Since I met Padre Pio, I can truthfully say that I have no doubts regarding Christ's being the Savior of the world."

Padre Pio was a man whose only desire in life was to please the Lord and to show his love for him every day. Padre Pio's journey home did not begin in the last days of his life; it began at the start of his life. A life that never for one moment was separated from the Lord!

REFLECTION

We have come to the end of our journey with Padre Pio. Has this journey of faith brought you closer to the Lord? As you read Carrigan's description of Padre Pio's Mass, which part spoke to you? The moment Padre Pio took off his gloves and Carrigan saw the wounds, he began a journey of faith that lasted the rest of his life.

In reading this account of Padre Pio's life, your journey is beginning, too.

Padre Pio suffered the Passion of Christ every day of his life for decades. Not one day went by when he didn't experience excruciating pain, beatings, and insults, and yet he gladly accepted it all for love of the Lord.

How does this speak to you? What do we suffer out of love for God? Do we accept the trials and suffering that come our way and offer them up to the Lord in thanksgiving for all that he has given us?

Carrigan was privileged to witness the Passion of Christ, and we are privileged to witness it through his eyes. When Carrigan kissed the wound on the hand of Padre Pio, did you feel the rigid edges of the wound as it brushed against his lips? Did you smell the fragrance of holiness? Did the bleeding of the wound move your heart for your beloved Lord?

As his friendship with Padre Pio developed over time, Carrigan truly drank from the Living Water. His faith was strengthened as he witnessed Padre Pio's great love for the Lord and willingness to embrace the Passion of Christ. Through Padre Pio, Carrigan came to know in his heart that Jesus *is* the Savior of the world.

Has your faith been strengthened by this journey?
How deep is your well?

PRAYER

May the Living Water who resides in my soul bring me refreshment and enrich my spiritual life.

Offer one Our Father, one Hail Mary, and one Glory Be.

NOTES

Introduction

1. "Birth and Childhood of Francesco Forgione in Pietrelcina," Caccioppoli Family website, www.caccioppoli.com.

2. "A Short Biography," Padre Pio Devotions, https://padrepiodevotions.org/a-short-biography/.

3. "A Short Biography."

4. "A Short Biography."

1. A River of Living Water

1. "Birth and Childhood of Francesco Forgione in Pietrelcina."

2. "A Short Biography."

3. Luigi Peroni, *Padre Pio da Pietrelcina* (Rome: Edizioni Borla, 2002), 23.

2. Padre Pio's Early Life and Visitations

1. Padre Pio da Pietrelcina, *Letters 3: Correspondence with His Spiritual Daughters* (San Giovanni Rotondo: Edizioni Padre Pio, 2012), 1006.

2. Padre Pio da Pietrelcina, *Letters 1: Correspondence with His Spiritual Directors* (San Giovanni Rotondo: Edizioni Padre Pio, 2011), 18.

3. "Birth and Childhood of Francesco Forgione in Pietrelcina."

4. "Fingerfood Biography of Padre Pio," Caccioppoli Family website, www.caccioppoli.com.

5. "Fingerfood Biography of Padre Pio."

6. "Fingerfood Biography of Padre Pio."

7. *Letters 1*, p. 528.

8. *Letters 1*, p. 17.

3. The Spiritual Gifts Revealed

1. You can also read about these gifts in *Iuvenescit Ecclesia*, a 2016 papal letter to the bishops of the Catholic Church, at vatican.va.

2. M. Winowska, *Il vero volto di Padre Pio* [The true face of Padre Pio] (Milan: Edizioni San Paolo, 1988), 134–35.

3. Autobiographical notes, *Letters 1*, p. 1425.

4. Mystical Touches

1. *Letters 1*, p. 211.

2. C. Bernard Ruffin, *Padre Pio: The True Story,* 2nd ed. (Huntington, IN: Our Sunday Visitor, 1991), 78–79.

3. Ruffin, *Padre Pio* (1991), 79.

4. *Letters 1*, p. 168.

5. *Letters 1*, p. 308.

6. *Letters 1*, p. 169.

7. *Letters 1*, p. 169.

8. *Letters 1*, p. 170.

5. Winds of Change

1. *Letters 1*, p. 1291.

2. Quoted in C. Bernard Ruffin, *Padre Pio: The True Story,* 3rd ed. (Huntington, IN: Our Sunday Visitor, 2018), 148. All subsequent citations refer to this edition.

3. *Letters 1*, p. 1186.

4. *Letters 1*, p. 1218.

5. *Letters 1*, p. 1206.

Notes 141

6. Paolo Carta, "Padre Pio's Love of Neighbor," EWTN, https://www.ewtn.com/catholicism/library/padre-pios-love-of-neighbor-13842.

7. Patricia Treece, *The Joyful Spirit of Padre Pio: Stories, Letters, and Prayers* (Cincinnati, OH: Servant Books, 2014), 11.

8. *Letters 1*, p. 1206.

9. *Letters 1*, p. 1206.

10. Carta, "Padre Pio's Love of Neighbor."

11. *Letters 1*, p. 1206.

6. Five Million Confessions

1. *Letters 1*, p. 1425.

2. Br. Michael Dimond, "Confessions with Padre Pio," December 31, 2006, vaticancatholic.com.

3. Fr. Stefano Manelli, *Padre Pio of Pietrelcina* (New Bedford, MA: Franciscans of the Immaculate), 89.

4. Fr. John A. Schug, *Padre Pio* (Chicago, IL: Franciscan Herald Press, 1983), 122.

5. Schug, *Padre Pio*, 122.

6. Franciscan Friars of the Immaculate, *Padre Pio: The Wonder Worker* (San Francisco, CA: Ignatius Press), 41.

7. Patricia Treece, comp., *Quiet Moments with Padre Pio: 120 Daily Readings* (Ann Arbor, MI: Servant Publications, 1999), no. 94.

8. John McCaffery, *Blessed Padre Pio* (Fort Collins, CO: Roman Catholic Books, 1999), p. 54.

9. Katharina Tangari, *Stories of Padre Pio* (Rockford, IL: TAN Books, 1996), 107–9.

10. Franciscan Friars, *Padre Pio: The Wonder Worker*, 30.

11. Tangari, *Stories of Padre Pio*, 50.

12. Ruffin, *Padre Pio*, 229.

13. Schug, *Padre Pio*, 230.

14. Ruffin, *Padre Pio*, 230.

7. Persecution and Confinement

1. Ruffin, *Padre Pio,* 181.

2. Padre Pio to Padre Bernardo Apicella, December 23, 1925, in *Letters 1.*

3. In *Padre Pio: The True Story,* C. Bernard Ruffin describes the confinement and persecutions of Padre Pio. I have used details from this book in this chapter.

4. *Letters 1*, p. 382.

5. Ruffin, *Padre Pio*, 159.

6. Ruffin, *Padre Pio*, 160.

7. Ruffin, *Padre Pio*, 210.

8. Ruffin, *Padre Pio*, 249.

9. Ruffin, *Padre Pio*, 257.

10. Ruffin, *Padre Pio*, 271.

11. "Pray, Hope, and Don't Worry" (newsletter), no. 69 (Autumn 2016), Padre Pio Devotions, https://padrepio devotions.org/newsletter-archives/.

8. Protection in Wartime

1. Ruffin, *Padre Pio*, 285.

2. Ruffin, *Padre Pio*, 283.

3. Ruffin, *Padre Pio*, 283.

4. Ruffin, *Padre Pio*, 284.

5. Ruffin, *Padre Pio*, 284.

6. Ruffin, *Padre Pio*, 290.

7. Ruffin, *Padre Pio*, 291.

8. Dorothy M. Gaudiose, *Mary's House: Mary Pyle: Under the Spiritual Guidance of Padre Pio* (New York: Alba House, 1992), 74.

9. Gaudiose, *Mary's House*, 74.

9. Maria L'Americana

1. *Letters 1*, 304.

2. Gaudiose, *Mary's House*, 30.

3. Gaudiose, *Mary's House*, 31.

4. Gaudiose, *Mary's House*, 34.

5. Gaudiose, *Mary's House*, 33.

6. Gaudiose, *Mary's House*, 76.

10. Padre Pio's Dream

1. Ruffin, *Padre Pio,* 322.

2. Ruffin, *Padre Pio,* 321.

11. Miracles and Recollections

1. *Letters 1*, p. 348.

2. "Testimony of Padre Agostino," Padre Pio Devotions, https://padrepiodevotions.org/testimony-of-padre-agostino/.

3. "He Was Not Expected to Live until Morning," Padre Pio Devotions, https://padrepiodevotions.org/testimonials/.

4. Ray Ewen, "A Blessed Rosary," Padre Pio Devotions, https://padrepiodevotions.org/a-blessed-rosary/.

5. Fanny Marro, personal recollection, May 5, 2023.

6. Fr. Paul Hancko, "I Received a Hand-Written Note from Padre Pio," Padre Pio Devotions, https://padrepiodevotions.org/testimonials/.

7. Padre Federico of Macchia Valfortore, "He Was Always Praying," Padre Pio Devotions, https://padrepiodevotions.org/he-was-always-praying/.

8. Jorge Contreras, Padre Pio Devotions, "My Doctor Said, 'What Have You Done?'" https://padrepiodevotions.org/my-doctor-said-what-have-you-done/.

9. Danilo Ganzon, "It Was Not Certain if I Would Live through the Night," Padre Pio Devotions, https://padrepio devotions.org/testimonials/.

10. Kenny Keegan, "I Thank Padre Pio from the Bottom of My Heart," Padre Pio Devotions, https://padrepiodevotions. org/i-thank-padre-pio-from-the-bottom-of-my-heart/.

11. "Pray, Hope, and Don't Worry" (newsletter), no. 69 (Autumn 2016), Padre Pio Devotions, https://padrepiode votions.org/newsletter-archives/.

12. The Journey Home

1. William M. Carrigan, "An Introduction to Padre Pio," EWTN, https://www.ewtn.com/catholicism/library/ introduction-to-padre-pio-5765.

Susan De Bartoli is the author of *Welcoming the Christ Child with Padre Pio* and serves as the secretary of the Board of Directors of the Padre Pio Foundation of America.

She has been a guest on various radio and television shows and podcasts, including *Let's Be Frank* and *Catholic Faith Network Live*.

De Bartoli is a pilgrimage tour operator and owner of Little Flower Pilgrimages. She also is assisting with the Cause for Canonization of Mary Pyle, Pio's assistant.

She attended Brooklyn College. De Bartoli is a lady commander of the Equestrian Order of the Holy Sepulchre of Jerusalem. She lives in the New York area.

littleflowerpilgrimages.com
Facebook: @susan.debartoli
Instagram: @susan_debartoli

DON'T MISS!

Welcoming the Christ Child with Padre Pio

DAILY REFLECTIONS FOR ADVENT

In *Welcoming the Christ Child with Padre Pio* by Susan De Bartoli, stories about the saint are woven with scripture and prayer to help you experience Advent—Padre Pio's favorite season—with greater hope and joy.

Each day includes daily readings, a quotation from Padre Pio, a short story about the saint, a scripture reflection, and a prayer to help you follow this extraordinary saint's example and welcome the Christ Child into your home and heart during Advent.